PARTING THE CURTAIN
An American Teacher in Postcommunist Romania

ANNE COE HEYNIGER

Five and Ten Press, Inc.
Washington, D.C.
2001

Parting the Curtain

DEDICATION

For Anca, Claudia, Claudiu, Dacian, Iancu,
Judith, Laci, Liana, Marcel, Mihai, Mirela,
Nicolae, Ovidiu, Radu, and Tudor,
who welcomed me.

"The most peaceful
place on earth is
among strangers."

— *Elias Canetti,*
Notes from Hampstead

A Transylvania farmer

INTRODUCTION

Timişoara (pron. Timischwara), a large provincial city in western Romania, was my home from April 1992 until July 1999. I went there originally for one year, at the request of a university president, to teach English. In those days, Americans and other foreigners did not go to Romania to work or play. Until Christmas Day 1989, the country had been for forty years in the grip of a ruthless communist dictator, Nicolae Ceauşescu (pron. show-shes-ku). On that day, the Romanians executed the dictator and his wife, making theirs the bloodiest revolution of the era. The country was impoverished and desperate.

By 1992, Americans had started going to Romania, but it was to adopt orphans. Romanian hearts were filled with hope and anticipation of freedom, a healthy economy and improved living standards. What they were getting were token improvements and slight nods to democracy. The bosses of the communist regime remained in power and were beginning to get rich. The events of Dec. 25, 1989 began to be characterized as a *coup d'état* rather than a revolution. *Democracy* was beginning to be equated with freedom to do whatever you liked and a new word had been added to the vocabulary — *profit*. It became a driving force, undergirded by acceptance of corruption in all its forms. The new visitors included few investors.

1

I stayed for seven years because I was happy there. My teaching afforded me great satisfaction. I made many friends of all ages. I discovered the pleasures of life in a small city where I walked and rode trams and stores closed at midday on Saturday afternoon so people could spend the weekend with their families. The country was "in transition" from communism to something else and, as a teacher, I was part of it.

My life before prepared me for Romania. Thanks to my parents, I had a liberal education and a small stock portfolio. My marriage to a foreign service officer took me to live in three Third World countries where I learned about deprivation, mostly other peoples'. I am good at languages, having learned several well enough to function in any situation. In Washington I had logged twenty years of professional experience in the nonprofit sector. My three children, now grown, were living the carefree single life and progressing in their professions. I had raised them as a single mother over two decades, and we were very close. But they no longer needed me. I was ready for something new.

During my Romania years, I returned to the U.S. for visits during school vacations, to be with my children and my father who was in his nineties. These visits were sweet. I was able to spend uninterrupted weeks with my dad and his caregivers. Although he was gradually succumbing to old age and dementia, he seemed to understand—more than anyone else—that my work in Romania was the reason for the light in my eyes, and he accepted it, even though it took me away from him for long periods. We liked to sit together in silence on the porch swing of his beach home. He was deaf and conversation was almost impossible, but the physical nearness was bonding and comforting to us both. My children were always glad to welcome me back, but my life in Romania was far removed from contemporary America and there were few points of congruence between their lives and mine. Even so, they each dedicated some of their precious vacation time to visiting me in Central Europe.

Parting the Curtain is mostly a memoir of my first year in Romania. The other six years contained many memories, but by then Timişoara had become my home and my work, and the details of daily life were no longer so different from life anywhere else. For the first four years, I kept a journal and wrote letters home on my laptop. In 1996, a student set me up for email and after that my thoughts and daily activities were sent through the ether, thence to the recycling bin. This memoir recounts my experiences, thoughts and feelings as I ventured into a land that, during most of my lifetime, had been hidden behind the Iron Curtain.

Anne and her dad, Bill Coe.

1 EASTWARD HO!

We were cruising at 35,000 feet over the Atlantic, headed for Paris. There I would change planes and board a Malev airliner for Budapest and Eastern Europe. In the hold, my luggage — 30 kg overweight — was stuffed with clothes for winter and summer, office supplies and a mini-drugstore of aspirin, prescription drugs, multi-vitamins, syringes and cosmetics. Scattered throughout the bags were brand new textbooks for teaching English as a second language, dictionaries, tapes of classical music, packets of dried soup and milk, instant coffee and tea, and my overseas "electronics": hot water heater, hair dryer, iron, tape/CD player. In the overhead compartment my precious laptop nestled in my new greatcoat.

It had come to me one afternoon in September 1991. I had just concluded a meeting with the head of a Romanian university, Radu Vladea. It was my responsibility to see visiting Romanians who showed up at the K Street office of the Citizens Democracy Corps. Usually visiting Eastern Europeans wanted to learn what our new agency could do for them. And usually I would offer them information — on U.S. organizations with programs in their country and individuals who wanted to volunteer. This gentleman — softspoken, warm, intense — spoke eloquently about his country.

"Romania," he said, "is greatly misunderstood in the West. With some help, it can overcome its communist past and again become the breadbasket of Europe and a valuable trading partner with the West. The potential is there. But we need Americans with us, among us. Americans are like water," he said. "They are life-giving."

"Life-giving?"

"Yes," he said. "They are proof that democracy works, that there is hope. We do not know this, as a people. We have been living in a nightmare for forty years, cut off, alone." He paused and looked at me intently. "We need you now...to be with us."

I didn't know what to say so I asked, "What about language? Can Romanians speak English?"

"No. We have studied but we cannot speak. We need teachers, people like you, to talk with us, to teach us about democracy. To show us what is democracy ."

As he spoke, I remembered a time in my life twenty years earlier. I was living in East Africa, the wife of a diplomat, and teaching English to working people and young male secondary school graduates. Those hours preparing lessons and teaching eager students had been among the most rewarding moments of my three years in Dar es Salaam. But that was another life. Another era.

Mr. Vladea smiled warmly and thanked me for my time. "I wait you in Timişoara," he said with a twinkle, stuffing booklets and pamphlets into his briefcase. "Goodbye."

I sat at my desk staring vacantly out the window at the deskbound man in the office building opposite. I had spent most of my daylight hours for the last twenty years in one Washington office or another. In this particular one we were supposed to be helping Eastern Europeans make the transition to democracy and a market economy. *Are we helping?* I wondered.

A few pencil figures on the back of an envelope told me that with some adjustments, and if I lived simply, I could forego my salary and live on my investment income. I could go to Romania. I would go to Romania. I walked into my colleague's office. She looked up expectantly.

"I'm going to Timişoara," I said.

―ᴇ―ᴇ―ᴇ

After Dulles and Charles de Gaulle airports, Budapest seemed like a landing strip in the bush. As I emerged from customs into an almost empty room, I saw a trio of people clustered around a handmade sign held aloft: "A. Heyniger." Two men and a woman greeted me warmly and explained that they worked with Mr. Vladea. They were Eugen, a research chemist from the Polytechnic, Gabriela, who was also a chemist and had a beautiful smile, and Florin, the driver, short, dark and handsome.

"You are welcome," said Gabriela. "We are glad you have come."

"*Bine aţi venit*," said Florin, who spoke only Romanian but who, I later learned, had a brother in Atlanta.

"It's wonderful to be here," I said, followed by one of the phrases I had learned from tapes. "*Mulţumesc.*" Thank you.

We jammed my five overstuffed bags into the small Romanian station wagon, and started south for the Romanian border, about 100 miles away.

Outside the countryside was boring — brown, flat farmland — but inside the car, the atmosphere was charged with excitement. Questions flew at me from all directions.

"Where do you live?" " How many rooms do you have?" "What does it cost?" "Is food expensive?" "Have you been to Las Vegas?" "Do you have a car?" "What kind?" "How much did it cost?" " Are people killed on the streets in Washington?" "Do you have husband?" "Do you have children?" "Do they live with you?" "Are you a teacher?" "Are there Indians in America?" "How long will you stay in Romania?"

I was beginning to wonder how politely to handle my fatigue and the barrage of questions.

We approached a long line of standing cars as the sun was setting.

"This is the border," said Eugen. "We may have some problems."

The line consisted of at least a hundred cars and trucks and nothing was moving. My carmates held an anxious discussion in Romanian. Suddenly Florin pulled the car out of line and drove rapidly to the front of the column. Here Gabriela got out and spoke to a man in uniform. Eugen said she was speaking Hungarian.

"She knows what to do," he said reassuringly.

Gabriela pointed to our yellow license plate (which signified an official government vehicle) and continued talking and smiling. The official peered through the window of the car, nodded and waved us on.

The Romanian customs was a hundred yards away. Again we went to the head of the line and Gabriela got out and spoke charmingly but authoritatively with the lone officer. Then we all got out and I could understand that they were discussing the official nature of our mission for the Polytechnic. I heard the words, "*profesoara de engleza*," several times, and "*america*." The customs officer walked over to me, looked me up and down, and asked rapidly, in Romanian, why I had come to Romania.

"To teach English." I replied. Gabriela translated.

"For how long?"

"One year."

"What is in the luggage?" he barked.

Thinking about the tape player hiding in the large suitcase, I said, "Clothes for one year, books and a radio."

"Open."

Fumbling with the tiny padlock and keys, I opened the huge duffel. The officer shone his flashlight inside and poked at the clothes on top.

Then he said, "Give me one book in English. For my daughter."

I looked at Gabriela.

"If you have...something..." she said, looking embarrassed.

I remembered packing a small picture book of Washington at the last minute. I rummaged in the outside pocket of the suitcase. It was there.

"Please," I said handing him the book. "I hope your daughter will enjoy this. How old is she?"

"She has five years. I keep it for her when she study English. You may go. *La revedere.*"

"*La revedere,*" we said in a chorus. I zipped up the bag trying to look calm. We piled back into the car.

"Welcome to Romania," said Gabriela.

"You were wonderful," I said.

She smiled. "I was nervous. But never mind. It is finished. And now we are going home."

The sun had set and we drove off in the growing darkness. Florin drove at high speed, navigating the potholes, passing huge lumbering trucks and horse-drawn wagons with no lights that sprang into our headlights at the last minute. Occasionally a Mercedes would overtake us and disappear into the night. I dozed.

When I opened my eyes, we were moving slowly through dark, silent city streets. I could see tall buildings and parked cars, but no people or other signs of life.

"Is this Timişoara?"

"No," said Eugen from the back seat. "This is Arad. There are still 50 kilometers until Timişoara."

I will never forget this first impression of a Romanian city: almost no lights; the streets seemingly uninhabited; above in the apartment buildings only an occasional light burning in a window.

"Why is it so dark?"

"Ah, but there is light," said Eugen, surprised. "Under Ceauşescu,* there were no lights at all. There was no electricity for the people. Only for the factories. But since the revolution, we have light."

Despite his explanation, the city looked deserted to me. I began to dread what Timişoara would be like.

It took an hour to get there. The outskirts of the city were one dark factory after another. The road widened and we began to pass rows of tall apartment buildings which resembled the grim apartment blocks in postwar Italian films. They all looked alike. There were more street lights now but few people, few cars and no neon lights beckoning us to a movie, a restaurant, a bar. The apartment blocks gave way to crumbling two- and three-story buildings with shuttered windows and closed gates. Darkened streetcars rumbled past us as we made our way through the narrow streets. The car slowed and stopped.

"We are in the center of the old city," said Gabriela. "Would you like to see it?"

"Oh, yes," I said and unfolded myself from the car.

We walked through a grove of trees and came out onto a broad open space that looked like a pedestrian mall. Moonlight flooded the square making everything visible but ghostly. In the center was a formal garden with flowers, silent fountains and benches. A few couples were strolling arm in arm. In the distance a sidewalk cafe with tables and umbrellas was a pool of light in the darkness. I felt the presence of a tall structure above us.

I looked up and saw spires reaching for the sky and moonlight shining on the ceramic tile roof.

"This is the Orthodox cathedral," said Eugen in a quiet voice. "It is very beautiful in the daytime. You will see tomorrow."

"And down there," he said, pointing to the other end of the square, "is the opera house."

"Do you have opera here?" I asked excitedly.

---

*This was the first of many comparisons people drew between present-day Romania and pre-revolutionary Romania. I would become sensitive to Romanians' need to explain their lack of modernity with these 'bad old days' contrasts.

"Oh, yes," he said, proudly. "Very fine opera. And now is the international music festival. There will be many concerts this month."

"And will you attend them?" I asked.

"Oh, no," said Eugen quickly, dismissing the idea. "It is too expensive. I have no time and too many problems to go to the concert. But you will go."

And I did. In the months ahead I would attend a symphony concert every Friday night and occasionally an opera.

Romania's first gift to me was music.

─⊘─⊘─⊘─

COŞ 104 (pronounced "kosh")*

A sleepy receptionist looked up as we entered the dimly lit lobby. She presided over a 1920s telephone board with an array of plugs. Gabriela explained who we were. The receptionist clanked two large keys on the counter.

"*Camera o-suta-patru,*" she said tersely. Room 104.

We quickly unloaded my bags from the car and carried them up a wide marble staircase covered with fraying carpet. There in the dark hallway my small emergency flashlight allowed us to find Room 104.

We surveyed the room in the light from an overhead bulb. It was about 10` by 12`, furnished with a narrow single bed, bedside table and lamp, glass-top table and chair, threadbare carpet, and a large mahogany wardrobe. A door and window opened onto a balcony. I walked out and looked down onto a quiet tree-lined street.

Opposite the wardrobe a beautiful sight greeted me: a green tile bathroom with a long, deep bathtub and a toilet the likes of which I hadn't seen since my first foreign travel to France at age 18. Stored in a well overhead, the water for the toilet was released by pulling a chain. A private bathroom! I couldn't believe my eyes.

It was nearly midnight and everyone was exhausted from the long drive. Gabriela said Radu Vladea, her boss and my sponsor, would come over in the morning. We embraced and said good night.

I was too tired to try the magnificent bathtub and just curled up on the little bed. Through the open window I could hear a bell tolling. Four gongs

*COŞ stands for Casa Oamenilor de Ştiinţă or, House of Men of Science

then twelve much deeper gongs. Midnight. That must be the cathedral, I thought. It was a comforting sound, very different from the police sirens of my Washington neighborhood. I fell asleep to the rhythmic *swishswish* of a streetsweeper's broom in the street below.

—☉—☉—☉

The Dining Room

Morning sun was streaming through the window when I opened my eyes and remembered where I was. *I am in Timişoara*, I thought. *I'm safe and all my belongings are here with me.* My partially opened duffels and suitcases were strewn about the floor.

I gazed around the room. Pretty much four walls, but OK. In the street men were calling to each other. Their language sounded lilting like Italian, then changed to a barking sound. Learning Romanian was going to be fun. It had been twenty years since I lived in another culture, learned another language.

Bathed and dressed in comfortable pants and a sweater, I ventured downstairs in search of breakfast. A new receptionist looked at me with curiosity.

"*Buna ziua*," I said, making a 'boona zeewa' sound.

"*Buna diminaţa*," she said. It sounded like 'boona deemeenatza'. (I learned later that this was the morning greeting used until 9:30 am.)

Pause. I didn't know how to say 'food.'

"*Unde* (where)…?" and I made an eating gesture with my hand.

"*Acolo*," she said, motioning me to the other end of the lobby.

So I went through two large doors into a large room. There were no people but many small square tables covered with clean white cloths. The only decor was several large plants — tropical trees with giant leaves straining at awkward angles toward the daylight which, in addition to a few small bulbs in the ceiling, provided the only illumination in the room. I sat down near the door. Places were set at several of the tables. I concluded there must be life here.

A young dark-haired waitress appeared. "*Buna ziua*," I said, looking up at her and smiling.

" '*Ziua*," she said tersely, not smiling.

From a grey metal pitcher she poured some liquid into my cup, then put before me a plastic basket with pieces of thick white bread and a plate containing salami slivers, two chunks of cheese, a tomato slice and a green onion. One pat of butter and a saucer of jam completed the breakfast. The liquid was hot sweet tea.

"*Camera?*" she inquired.

When I looked blank, she said it louder. "*Camera*...CAMERA," she barked.

I realized she was asking about my room and fished in my pocket for the key. She scribbled something on a note pad and left. I devoured the bread, butter and jam, the cheese and tomato. I left the salami, onion and tea.

I would come to hate that room.

It was curiously devoid of any aesthetic pleasure associated with eating. The people responsible for service seemed to enjoy making as much noise as they could — dragging chairs and tables across the room with a loud scraping sound, and shouting back and forth to each other in the kitchen to the accompaniment of clanging pots and pans.

After I had been there a week or so, a waitress might occasionally smile at me, especially after I began to speak a little Romanian. When that happened it would set the tone for my whole day. But the food served was always unappetizing and always the same. Sometimes at breakfast the bread would be toasted — at the discretion of the waitress who was on. Lunch, the main meal of the day, consisted of mashed potatoes or rice and meat swimming in a pale gravy. Sometimes there was a cabbage or tomato salad, swimming in dressing. I began to realize that for the first time in my life I might be hungry.

That is exactly what happened.

~~⊙~⊙~⊙~~

An Invitation

On my way back to my room I saw a familiar figure standing at the front desk. It was Radu Vladea, the rector of the Polytechnic University, in blue jeans and a sweat shirt. When he saw me he beamed and held out his hand.

"Ah, I see you have really come to us," he said in his deep voice.

"Yes. I am finally in Romania. Thank you for sending your staff to meet me yesterday. I like them."

"Is everything OK?" he asked quietly, looking at me intently. "Your room? the food? Have you problems?"

"No problems."

"Very well. Today is what in the States you would call a holiday. It is Easter. You're surprised, of course. You see, the Orthodox Easter is always later than the Roman Easter and most Romanians are Orthodox. So there is nothing to do here for the next four days. Would you like to go with my family to the mountains for a few days? It is not very far. I think it will be interesting for you."

I thought of my luggage and belongings strewn about the room waiting for me to bring order to the chaos, of my promise to call home, of my fatigue, of my engagement book so necessary in Washington. But that book had blank pages for the rest of the year.

"How lovely. Thank you."

I joined Radu, as he asked me to call him, in his tiny car. He exuded energy and drove rapidly. I stole a look at this man who had inspired me to travel halfway around the world and who stood between me and complete anonymity. As in Washington, he radiated confidence, sincerity...and empathy. He understood how strange I was feeling and was taking me into the bosom of his family. His smile and warmth put me completely at ease. I didn't have to worry about anything, even my most valuable possessions which were in the money belt tight around my waist and in the computer case under my arm. All was perfectly safe. I trusted Radu completely.

We drove the short distance to his apartment. It was in a 'block' of flats. Six stories. Inside I was reminded of public housing projects in Washington: dark hallways, the smell of damp cement and cooking, iron railings, stairs to climb.

On the top floor, a beautiful woman in her mid-thirties with black hair and olive skin stood in an open door.

"Welcome, Anne," she said quietly. "I am Claudia."

2 second Day

Claudia was Radu's wife. I knew that she had been his student and now worked in a chemistry lab. With her today were her two young children. They looked like twins; each had their mother's straight black hair cut in a Dutch boy bob. They peeked out from behind their mother, nudging each other.

"I am Radu," said the boy, stepping forward, standing tall. "I am the oldest." He was about 10, with large dark eyes and a serious look.

"I am Raluca," said his sister, looking at the floor.

"And my name is Anne," I said, kneeling down to look into their faces. "I'm from America."

"We know," they sang in a chorus and ran from the tiny hall into an adjoining room.

We followed the children into the room in which an oval dining room table with high-backed carved wood chairs occupied most of the space. Dominating the room was a TV tuned loud to a children's program in German. The children crowded each other into an armchair to watch.

"Please," said Radu Vladea, offering me a straight-back chair. He and Claudia left the room, closing the door behind them. With the children absorbed in the program I took the opportunity to look around the small room. The door to a narrow balcony let in the sun. Two elaborately carved glass cabinets of highly polished wood held dishes, crystal and china figurines. This was obviously the main room of the apartment. Radu returned quietly and sat at the head of the table. I noted that everyone but me was in stocking feet.

"You can see, we live simply here," he began. "We have not so many rooms as you do in America." He knew this because he had visited my spacious Washington apartment during the winter. I was uncomfortable with the comparison and changed the subject.

"Do your children understand German?" I asked.

"Yes, they are fluent," said Radu proudly. "They are both in the third grade at a German school."

"And their English?"

"They study a little," he said. "But they are shy to speak. You must encourage them to speak."

Claudia returned, closing the door after her. She brought small cups of coffee, dishes of sliced cheese, salami, bread and butter and a cut-up kiwi.

"*La masã, copii*," said Claudia. The children tore their attention from the TV to sit at the table. The TV stayed on.

I was hungry. The coffee was aromatic and strong. I wondered where we were going, and how I would communicate with my companions since only Radu senior actually spoke English. Claudia and her children were speaking Romanian at what seemed a very fast clip.

"Where are we going, Radu?" I asked.

"To a small village in the mountains, about 200 kilometers from here. It was a German village but all the Germans have left back to Germany and there are many empty houses. The air is very clean there. But it will be cold. Have you something warm?"

"Oh, yes. But I have no dress. Will I need a dress?"

He chuckled and looked at Claudia. "Oh, no. What you are wearing is fine. The house is...how shall I say....quite simple."

The doorbell rang and Claudia rose to answer it, closing the door behind her. Voices in the hallway. A man and woman in their late thirties entered. Each embraced Radu and the children with a quick hug, touching both cheeks. Then they turned to me.

"I'm Anne Heyniger," I said since introductions did not seem to be forth-coming, "*Buna ziua.*"

"I am Laura," said the pretty blonde woman in English. She had dancing eyes and bright red lipstick. "Welcome to Romania."

"I am Mario," said the man. He was slim and handsome with curly hair and a slightly mischievous look. "We are glad you have come." We shook hands.

I was relieved that both appeared fluent in English. "Thank you," I said. "You speak English beautifully."

"We are both teachers," said Mario.

"In a school?"

Laughing, "No, no. We give private lessons. After our work. To make some money. We are all very poor here. You will see," he said knowingly and offered me a Marlboro. "Do you smoke?" I shook my head and everyone took advantage of the moment to light up.

Laura said wistfully, "I was in the States once. Last year. For two weeks. It was beautiful…beautiful." She looked off into the distance and I thought she might cry. "I would have stayed if I did not have Mario and Bianca. But…I came back, didn't I?" and she gave her husband, who was smiling wryly, a gentle tap.

"Since she went to the States, everything here looks bad," said Mario. "And everything here IS bad," he added, laughing at his joke. "Just wait. You will see."

By now the room was thick with smoke, but it was time to go. Claudia and Laura produced covered dishes and baskets of food, luggage, rolls of toilet paper, tennis rackets and balls, and we all descended to the parking lot where two small beaten-up Dacias* were waiting. I was invited to ride in the car with the women. To my dismay, Radu said he had to stay in Timişoara and could not accompany us. A university election was coming up and his job was on the line.

I would spend most of the next few days talking with or through the two teachers. Because although the beauteous Claudia seemed to understand most of what Laura and I were saying, she rarely ventured to speak. When I began teaching I would find this to be the norm. My students could read English and translate, and they knew grammar, but they could not speak the language. Their opportunities to listen to the spoken language had been limited to movies and rock music. And there was something else at work. It wasn't just shyness. It seemed like fear of failure, of appearing foolish.

I began to understand why Radu had wanted me to come.

-⊘-⊘-⊘-

*Dacia is the name of the small four-cylinder car made in Romania by a state company. The name comes from the ancient kingdom of Dacia, centered in western Transylvania, which existed until AD 107, when it was conquered by the Romans.

An Easter Excursion

The road took us quickly out of town. Ducks and geese scattered as we sped through village after village where the houses appeared to be joined in an endless fence. Once or twice I caught sight of a huge pig lying in the ditch or strolling about. Women in kerchiefs, heavy skirts and clogs chatted on benches in front of their houses, their children playing around them.

Rounding a bend, we slowed down and Laura pointed to a tiny structure of twigs on top of a utility pole. "Storks," she said. "They come every year to this very same spot and there are always babies in the early summer." Indeed I could see the head of a stork sticking out of the nest. Was it a mother stork sitting on her eggs?

I remembered Marguerite de Angeli's story about a stork family that returned to the same village nest year after year. At that moment I felt as if I were the character in a story...my story...going backward in time.

We began to climb. Forests of fir trees stretched away on both sides of the road. Above the green mantle were snow-covered peaks. Peering out the car window I saw a swift-running stream in the valley below. Around a curve where the stream widened into a river, a dam destroyed the beauty of the valley. Close by was a deserted factory, its smokestacks reaching for the sky, surrounded by ugly blocks of flats.

The road became a steep rock-strewn track. We were driving uphill at a 45-degree angle through a village of tiny storybook houses with peaked roofs, lace curtains at the windows and tightly shut gates. Some of the houses had two sets of initials painted into the gable. Laura said they were the names of the man and wife who built the house. "This is Gãrãna. It was a German village called Wolfsberg but the communists renamed it," she said, "and now the Germans all left." I asked why. "Because now they can leave. Before, the Romanians forbid it. Now, although Romanians are not welcome in Germany, if you are an ethnic German you can get in. At least for now."

She explained that after independence, the Romanian economy worsened and many of the German-Romanians went for good to Germany, leaving behind houses and fields and sometimes even animals in the barns.

Our car slowed and stopped in front of one of the doors, No. 27. Everyone piled out, delighted to be out of the car. The children raced down the steep hill, throwing a tennis ball. Mario unloaded the suitcases and the buckets and dishes of food which he carried through the old metal gate into an interior grassy space open to the sky. The house was built in a square around this simple courtyard.

Inside, the little house was dark and musty with low ceilings. The sleeping rooms were crowded with several beds that had been pushed together and piled high with comforters. Dusty curtains hung at the tiny paned windows. In the kitchen the main feature was an ancient wooden structure with a hatch-like cover and a large wheel. A well. Laura showed me how to get a drink by rotating the wheel, which lowered a bucket to the dark pool twenty feet below. I turned the wheel tentatively. The water was cold and sweet.

To my surprise, there was electricity. A single light bulb hung from the ceiling and there was a two-burner electric stove but no refrigerator. Water was drawn from the well since there was no indoor plumbing. The outhouse was behind the empty animal stalls.

Laura and Claudia set about heating up the food they had prepared at home. Over the next two days we had one feast after another — specialties for Easter. Lamb soup, sheep cheese, sausages of every description, minced pork, sweetbreads baked with herbs and breadcrumbs, corn meal mush topped with sour cream and poached eggs. And throughout the day and night, beer, wine and a fiery homemade brandy made from plums called *ţuica* (pron. sweeka).

The women spent most of their holiday in that kitchen, heating food and water, chopping vegetables and washing dishes while the children played tennis in the road and roamed the hillsides of Gărăna. I sat outside with Mario at a card table in the grassy space, enjoying the sunshine, drinking strong coffee in little cups, and smoking. I was not allowed to help with anything; the women waited on me and Mario. Mario had brought his tape deck. We listened to his collection of American rock music.

One afternoon the whole group walked up the hill to visit with some friends from Timişoara who were also spending the Easter holiday in Gărăna. The friends were a married couple who were both doctors, their parents, and a pre-teenager. We sat outside in the garden around a table, enjoying the pure air, drinking strong coffee. For my benefit, the conversation was in French since that was the language educated people used to study and I had spoken French all my life.

At a certain moment, a radio was turned on and we heard Radio Free Europe describing the dramatic visit of the exiled Romanian King Mihai to Bucharest. This was the first time the king had been allowed to visit, and be welcomed by an ecstatic crowd, since his exile in 1947. No Romanian radio station was permitted to carry the live coverage. RFE reported a hundred thousand people had gathered in the city's main square to greet the aging former king who lives simply and quietly in Switzerland. My companions expressed sadness that the monarchy would probably never be restored, condemning Romania to a future of corrupt politicians and discord. The cheering and excitement of the crowd washed over us. No one spoke.

After a while, the oldest gentleman at the table broke the silence, asking me in French, "And what are your initial impressions of our country?"

I thought a moment. "I feel myself transported back in time to another age *(époque),*" I said. "I think I will be happy here."

Although my brain was bombarded with impressions, this was, thankfully, a relaxing time for my body. Jet lag had set in, along with culture shock. No one seemed to mind when I disappeared to sleep or read in my huge featherbed, or go for a walk to stretch my stiff muscles. Mario joined me on one of these. We walked uphill, past the deserted houses, each with a garden or orchard in back sloping steeply to the river below. There were no people.

As we trudged upward, Mario began to talk, slowly at first, then the words came tumbling out. He said the abandoned village reminded him of Romania. This was my first exposure to the disgust many Romanians felt about their lives, their leaders, their future. Their hopelessness and despair stood in stark contrast to the excitement of discovery that I was feeling.

Despite his cynicism, Mario liked to laugh and joke and flirt. We found many points of contact, of overlapping experience and interests. We found that we both love music, especially classical music, and that weekend my instruction in rock music began (which my students later continued). Mario also had a keen interest in relationships, similar to my American friends who have been in therapy, and I found myself sharing with him some aspects of my life that I rarely speak about.

Over the next two days we ate heartily in mid-afternoon, slept, took walks, heated well water for sponge baths, and at night, bundled in our comforters against the cold, watched "Jesus of Nazareth" on a tiny black and white TV.

Easter morning we drove to a lake and poked around a boarded-up motel complex whose owners had left the country. There was a dining room, a wide terrace and beached paddle boats. "Three Waters," as the resort was called, had touristic possibilities but it was clear anyone taking it over would have to spend a great deal of money renovating it.

From the lake we climbed to the top of the mountain and found a ski lodge, complete with lift, sun deck and a children's playground. Everything was rusting and rotting. Trash littered the hillside, but through the thin crust of snow on the ground, tiny purple crocuses pushed their faces to the sun. The children ran about delightedly gathering them and with shy formality presented me with two huge bunches of blooms. "*Cristos a înviat!*" they said smiling, arms outstretched. "Christ has risen," said Mario and completed the Easter exchange saying softly, "*Adevarat a înviat!* He has risen indeed!"

At the summit, commanding a view of the valley and neighboring peaks, stood a small chapel with a belltower. I approached and pushed open the carved wood doors. Inside it was dark and still. I was alone. A faint aroma of incense hung in the air. Looking down I saw I was treading on Persian carpets and quickly removed my muddy shoes. On the altar, the burnished metal halos of icons reflected flickering light from candles in crimson glass holders. Images of saints, angels and devils in brilliant reds, blues and gold covered the walls. In a metal bin near the entrance, stubs of votive candles stood in a pool of hardened wax. I fished for matches in my purse, selected a candle and, saying a prayer for my darling sister who died in 1988, lit it and placed it in the bin. Then I put a hundred-lei note in the candle box and climbed to the belltower for a view. The bell rope was waiting. I pulled it once, twice. The bell clanged across the peaks announcing my presence and Easter Day.

Rezi

A Vladea family ritual during their holidays in Gărâna was to fetch milk, cream and eggs from one of the remaining farmers in the village. Easter Monday morning I joined Claudia and the children on this errand. The farmer in this case was an eighty- year-old German woman named Rezi who also owned the house we were staying in. When we appeared at the door, a tiny woman in a scarf looked up at us, cocked her head, smiled broadly and invited us in.

We crowded into her parlor. The main decoration was a 1989 wall calendar and a color picture of the crucified Christ. Claudia and I were offered thimblefuls of țuica. The children had foaming glasses of milk from the cow that was standing just outside the door in the courtyard. We ate cookies from a tin box. The Easter greeting was repeated. "*Cristos a înviat!*" said Rezi and we replied, "*Adevarat a înviat!*"

I wanted to paint Rezi. I couldn't stop looking at her face. It was wrinkled and brown from the sun, eyes a piercing blue, teeth white and straight, cheeks ruddy. Her hands were gnarled and arthritic and she had a slight limp. She laughed a lot. There was something mischievous about her, as if she had a secret. She had a look that was…knowing. And she kept looking at me with frank, good-humored curiosity. I wanted to find out everything about her and her life. But that was impossible. We were speaking a mixture of German, Romanian and English and I contributed little to the conversation.

Her clothes were those of a peasant — headscarf, embroidered vest, heavy pleated skirt of coarse material, warm socks and wooden clogs. She looked as if she spent most of her life out-of-doors. (In fact I saw her again that afternoon as we were leaving Gărăna. She was clearing a field for spring planting by burning the grass, beating out the fire with a pitchfork when it got too close to the fruit trees, coaxing flaming grasses down the hillside.)

I learned later that Rezi is considered wealthy. She never married and owns several farms which she works herself. At the end of our visit she presented Claudia with enough milk and eggs for a week at no charge, since it was Easter. From her doorway, Rezi waved goodbye to us as we descended the rocky downhill path.

I was beginning to feel welcome. And safe. In this remote village I had learned something about hospitality. And I was beginning to ask myself questions: Is there anything in my Washington life comparable to this? Have I been confusing hospitality with showing off my home and possessions? Who helps the stranger in my city survive the traffic, the filled calendars, the stress, the fear of crime? Why am I so happy to be here?

—ⓖ—ⓖ—ⓖ—

Alone

"Goodbye...*la revedere*...thank you so much...*mulţumesc frumos*...good-bye!"

Car doors slammed. The children waved goodbye to me and suddenly I was alone. It was getting dark. The lobby was empty and dimly lit. I climbed the stairs to my room, turned on the two small lights and surveyed the scene. Winter and summer clothes piled on the floor; fleece-lined boots, sandals, plastic bags with syringes and prescription medicines, new paperbacks, textbooks, stacks of cassettes in their plastic boxes, a few CDs, packets of dried soup, blocks of Hershey chocolate in the familiar brown paper with silver letters. A bottle of scotch.

Panic lurks. My inner friend says 'Don't give in. It's time to take action.' I dig out the Magnavox from its nest in the huge suitcase, check the eight batteries and select a tape. It works. Music fills the room. Elizabeth Schwarzkopf is singing a Ricard Strauss 'Last Song.' I pour some scotch in a glass, rationing it, and add some water from the bottle on the table. Thank goodness I packed a bottle opener. I sip. I am doing familiar things. I check the voltage switch on the electric pot, fill it with tap water and plug it into the outlet. When it begins to bubble I rummage in the piles on the floor and unearth a packet of asparagus soup. Then I breathe deeply several times. Supper tonight will be asparagus soup, chocolate and whiskey.

3 NIGHT THOUGHTS

I am awakened in the middle of the night by the streetsweeper just below my balcony. I get up quietly to watch him. Swish, swish, swish goes his broom of twigs, and then the loud metallic clank of his shovel as he scoops and dumps into his ancient wheelbarrow. He is leaning on his shovel. Why does he do this at night? Doesn't he realize the noise he's making?

I've seen a lot of people doing this kind of work. In every park there seems to be a small, slow-moving group of women in bandannas and heavy denim skirts, mostly older women — but not all — who are snipping hedges, pulling up weeds and putting in plants. Men cut the tall grass with scythes.

Why is there so much trash everywhere, despite the women? On every corner there's a dumpster filled with trash, sometimes burning.

20

People use the parks much more than at home. They sit on the dilapidated park benches, which for some reason are only 18 inches off the ground, and eat lunch, embrace, visit, or do nothing. There are lots of old people on the benches. And some vagrants.

I like the Rose Park two blocks from my hotel. There are thousands of rose bushes there, planted in formal geometrical arrangements. Soon they will be in bloom. Someone told me the city parks were designed in the first quarter of the century with sculpture and fountains. But all that remains of the sculpture are the pedestals and the fountains no longer play. Along the river bank there are weeping willows and stately poplars. It's all so elegant, but decaying. It makes me sad.

In "my" park there's also an outdoor amphitheatre with seats for about a thousand people. Yesterday I heard loudspeakers from there blaring the Lord's Prayer. It was being sung in English. What on earth? I went to see. An American evangelist was holding a kind of revival.

I ran away.

—6—6—6

Victories

In those first weeks, each day brought at least one small victory. The purchase of a table knife was the first. I found it at a department store in the center of town. This required finding my way from the hotel to the town center, deciding which store was most likely to have knives, and making the purchase with *lei*, a currency that operated in the hundreds and thousands. Store window displays were not helpful. They contained totally unrelated items — canned peas, perfume, Marlboro cigarettes, pyramids of toilet paper rolls and Pepsi Cola cans, plastic toys, cooking oil, a child's backpack. After several mistakes, I chose one store — *Materna* — and sure enough it had some household items. Through pantomime I was able to convey what I wanted to a bored salesgirl and purchased a serrated aluminum knife with plastic handle made in the USSR.

At the corner a man was selling fresh bread and I bought a long *baguette*. In a store with items in the window I purchased a kilogram of butter and a jar with fruits on the label which turned out to be what I wanted — jam. Heading back to the hotel I passed another street vendor selling small cans of Nescafe and large red and white plastic Marlboro bags (*punga*). I returned to the hotel carrying my purchases in my *punga*. Just having a *punga* made me fit in more with the scenery since everyone on foot carried some kind of bag. Once in my room I happily set about preparing for breakfast on my sunny balcony.

Even though I'm not a nutritionist, I knew that something was wrong with my diet. I had not knowingly eaten a green vegetable since my dinner on the plane. That day I had seen some children in the park peeling an orange, so there was fruit somewhere, but I didn't know where to find it. When Eugen came to check on me, as he did every day, I asked if we could buy some fruit and vegetables. He said we could go to the market the next day.

That afternoon at the 2:00 meal, knowing that I would soon have an alternative source of food, I felt less at the mercy of the waitresses who ruled the dining room. My self-confidence was growing daily and I was beginning to use standard Romanian phrases that sometimes brought giggles, but more often, a smile and words of encouragement.

⌀─⌀─⌀.

The Market

The tram stopped and emptied its passengers into a roiling sea of bodies and noise. Eugen and I, each carrying two sturdy plastic bags, began inching our way along the perimeter of the market scene. I held fast to his arm, my purse pressed hard between my upper arm and torso. Women and men jostled each other trying to make headway through the throng. Unshaven men with wool sweaters buttoned tightly against the early morning chill. Children with frightened eyes and round heads encased in woollen caps clutching their mothers' skirts. Old people with humped backs leaning on canes. Stocky women, their determined colorless faces framed by scarves.

Everyone seemed to be clothed in brown or grey, a contrast to the tables laden with piles of onions, carrots, peppers, apples, potatoes, bananas and small hills of cabbages — an artist's palette of primary colors. Behind the tables the farmers lounged, sipping hot tea or beer, smoking and laughing with their neighbors. Potential customers asked repeatedly *Cit costa?* to which the vendors snapped out a price, usually the same as their neighbor's. Some vendors were selling from cloths spread on the ground, many of them dark-skinned women wearing brightly colored sweaters, full skirts and heavy gold jewelry, with a child at the breast. "Gypsies," said Eugen. "Be careful. They will steal your money." (see Appendix 2, Gypsies)

Turning my attention from the gypsies to Eugen, I said, "I want to buy some apples, lettuce, tomatoes, onions and cucumbers. Maybe some carrots. And oranges."

"Very well. You must select carefully," said Eugen and guided me to a table. I chose, placing my items in the metal bin on the farmer's scale. He announced the weight and the price of each binful. Eugen paid, and the farmer poured the purchases into my *punga*. Eugen said it wouldn't do any good to bargain. If we didn't like the price we could buy elsewhere.

I was beginning to understand the sound of some key Romanian phrases — *oh soota* for one hundred; *tray soota chin zech* for three hundred and fifty; *bookat* for piece; *kit kosta* for how much. There did not seem to be many polite phrases being exchanged between buyer and seller. No 'good morning,' 'how are you,' 'please,' or 'thank you.' Everyone acted as if they had very little time, even the sellers, who presumably would be standing in the same spot all day. Once I said *mulțumesc* (thank you) to a large healthy-looking farm woman who sold me four large healthy-looking carrots, and she smiled broadly and inquired if I was German. When Eugen said, "*Nu, e americanca,*" she was clearly amazed and said, "*Bine ați venit!*" (welcome), to which I replied, "*Mulțumesc,*" smiled and shook her hand.

Back at the Coș, Eugen and I celebrated our success at the market by consuming two succulent oranges on my balcony, followed by a thimbleful of scotch.

—◦—◦—◦.

Communications

It was clear that communication with the outside world was going to be a problem. I had not spoken to anyone in the States since arriving two weeks earlier. The antiquated Timișoara telephone system could not handle modern telecommunications. Just getting a dial tone on my vintage 1920 instrument was an achievement. Then the connection might or might not be made and it might or might not be the right number. If I was lucky enough to actually talk to someone, I knew we could be cut off at any moment and I would have to start all over again.

One day, after many hours of trying, I finally reached my sister in Boston in the middle of her night. We quickly completed an agenda of necessary items in case of a cutoff, then just spoke quietly about nothing special, savoring the sound of each other's voice, as the vast expanse of mountains, ocean and sky that separated us melted away and the threads of familiarity and love drew us together. There were tears in my eyes when we hung up. Tears of love, not loneliness.

-◎-◎-◎.

Routines

My days were beginning to assume some structure. Up at 7, hot bath in the grand tub, breakfast in the hated dining room, augmented by my carry-in fruit. An hour with my Romanian tapes, letter writing, a couple of hours exploring the city on foot, locating shops and devising routes. An hour translating a news story from one of the many local papers. Lunch at 2 o'clock in the dining room now crowded with students eating quietly in groups of four.

Every day the meal was the same: clear soup with floating vegetable bits, chunks of pork covered with gravy, potatoes or rice, sometimes a boiled vegetable, mineral water and coffee. I dreaded the meal, which was filling but tasteless and which I ate at a table alone. But I liked watching my fellow diners, some of whom might soon be my students.

They were mostly dark, long-haired young men, unshaven, wearing jeans, t-shirts and sneakers. Their faces were sensitive and passionate. No one resembled an American "jock." Most looked pale and unhealthy. They ate ravenously, heads close to their plates, talking little. No raucous laughter or horseplay such as one might see in an American college dining room. And no books. I had expected to see students loaded down with books as they traversed the city between classes and I wondered where they had left them.

I soon found out. They had none.

-◎-◎-◎.

Books & Teaching Assignment

The moment I had been waiting for finally arrived. Radu phoned one morning to say I had an appointment at the "faculty" to discuss my teaching. The meeting was to take place at the *rectorat*, an imposing building in the center of town, ten minutes' walk from my room. The Polytechnic had no campus to speak of. Its buildings were scattered throughout the city.

The head of the English department at the Polytechnic, whose name was Rodica, greeted me with a smile tinged with a certain reserve. She was a good-looking woman of about 35, trim and well-dressed. Her English was flawless. She chose and pronounced each word as if she were being interviewed on TV. After a few pleasantries she asked if I would like to meet students. I said yes, and we entered a classroom where 25 young men were bent over their desks writing. They were second-year chemistry students.

Rodica introduced me as the new American lecturer and I was on. To get them talking, I asked what they knew about the U.S. At first they were reluctant to speak and I labored for responses. But after ten minutes we were laughing and making jokes about rock music, cars, movies and sports. As we left the classroom, Rodica said matter-of-factly that she was sure all her students would want me for a teacher. I said that was flattering but I didn't think it was fair to compare, since I was a novelty. But I was encouraged. I had sensed their surprise, curiosity and good will.

Rodica assigned me five groups — two from the chemistry faculty, two from mechanical and one from electrical engineering. Over one hundred students, mostly boys. Each group would meet once a week for two hours. So ten class hours a week. It didn't seem like enough, for me or the students. They had not had a regular English teacher or class since the end of the first semester, when three teachers from the department left for training in England. My arrival seemed timely.

I asked about books. Rodica showed me a locked bookshelf in the English office with one row of textbooks behind glass.

"You may borrow these, but they are only for you. They are not for students. You will have to write on the blackboard," she said tartly. "We used to have more books in our library but most of them have been stolen. We try to prevent this but it is very difficult. You must be very careful."

"What about a copier?"

"I believe there is a shop in the center where you may make copies. But it is very expensive. Ask the students. They will know where it is. But you will be teaching them conversation and correcting their grammar. Why will you need copies?"

Since I had no idea what I would be teaching, I was unable to answer.

"May I look at the textbooks?" I asked.

"Of course. Just tell the secretary to lock the office's security grill when you are finished. And ask her for a schedule. I must return to my class. Here is my home telephone number. Call me if you have any questions. Goodbye, Anne." She gave me her business card and left.

The dimensions of my task were beginning to emerge: teach English to a hundred engineering students of varying English proficiency without the benefit of books or copier and probably little input from other teachers. Fortunately I had brought a few new textbooks with me, and there were some good ones here. Also I had my tape deck and tapes. Most important of all, I had a powerful urge to get started.

4 TEACHER

They sat with their heads down, eyes lowered, to avoid being called on. A few had come early and occupied the front row of desks, eager to be heard and to dominate this, my very first class. Behind them, their silent classmates glanced at me surreptitiously, wrote notes to each other, read magazines. When one of these was asked to speak he complied grudgingly but in such a tiny voice I had to ask him to repeat and speak clearly.

It was obvious that these students were not used to participating. Most of them appeared to be terrified of speaking in class...in any language. (I soon learned from students that in Romanian universities professors lecture, students take notes and discussions or questions are rare.) In those first hours, my overarching goal became to get my students to speak, to use the language they had been studying for years with their Romanian teachers.

In this and subsequent classes, the range of the students' language proficiency was vast — monosyllabic to fluent — and all were unused to asking questions. So I would begin those first classes with,

"I know you have some questions you would like to ask me. Please ask them." Slowly, interest would begin to flicker in their faces.

Student in a tiny voice: "Where do you live?"

"Washington, D.C. What do you know about Washington, D.C.?"

A voice, softly, "It's the capital of the United States."

"Good. Your turn."

"Where is your husband?"

"I'm divorced. Keep going."

Another voice: "Do you have a machine in Washington?"

"A machine? What kind of machine?"

Another student: "He means, a CAR."

"Oh. Yes, I do."

"What is it?"

"A Chevrolet."

Another student: "Is it a sports car?"

"No. It's a cheap model. What *does* that mean anyway, *cheap*?" No one answered.

I wrote *cheap* on the board and someone said *less money*.

"Good. That's close. *Cheap* means *little* money. What's another word for cheap?"

No one answered. I put *inexpensive* and *expensive* on the board.

What does expensive mean?"

Much money came the answer.

"Good. And *inexpensive* means little money. What's the Romanian word for *cheap* or *inexpensive*?"

The answer came but was unintelligible. I asked a boy in the front row to write it on the board. A boy with a ponytail and tattered denim jacket obliged. Everyone wrote in their books.

"OK, what else would you like to ask me?"

"Have you any children?"

"Yes, I do. Three. (pause) Ask another question."

"Boys or girls?"

"I have two boys and one girl. The girl is tall and blonde with blue eyes" (Wolf calls from the rear.) I smile. "She teaches handicapped teenagers in a high school. The oldest boy is a journalist. The youngest boy is a salesman."

Hand goes up. "What's a salesman?"

I ask for an answer from the class.

(Tentatively) "He sells in a shop?"

"No, he doesn't sell in a shop. He works for a large corporation and his job is to sell the products of that company to other companies. He spends his days wearing a coat and tie making sales calls."

"What means *sales calls*?"

"A sales call is when you go out and visit someone in their workplace, and try to sell them your product." And I wrote the correct way to ask the question on the board (*What does 'sales call' mean?*) and asked several to repeat it.

I began writing words on the board and the rest of the hour was spent in an ever-expanding discussion of selling, companies, working conditions, competition, profit and sales commissions, most of which was new to my budding engineers. Maybe they didn't understand every word I said, but I had their attention. Every eye was on me; the shyness was gone.

From the back of the room came, "Please, can you tell me what is the meaning of *dire straits?*"

I asked him where he had heard this phrase.

"It's a rock group…and a great one."

I had never heard of it. "OK. You use the phrase, *dire straits* when you want to say something is in very bad shape, in a bad way. For example, 'the economy of Romania is in dire straits.' (laughter)

"I would like to hear this group. Does anyone have a tape of the Dire Straits?" Several hands went up. "OK. If you will lend me your tape, I will lend you a tape called *Anne* (that's me) *Rocks Romania*", which my son made for me before I came here, with all the newest rock hits. Do I have a deal?"

I did.

"By the way. I'd like you to call me Anne. And I'll call you by your first names. OK?"

Thus began a cultural exchange that would bring me closer to my students than anything else I did in those early days. For music — rock music (not my usual choice) — had penetrated the Iron Curtain. My students knew the words and music of countless rock songs. Many had learned their English from them. Videos, books and magazines were too expensive for the average student, but audio tapes were affordable and available. Almost every student had a cassette player. Several were musicians who either played in a band or sang in a choral group. I decided to bring music into the classroom.

Back in my hotel room I listened to my tape of Bob Dylan's "Blowin' in the Wind" several times and wrote down the words, filling a piece of paper with three sets of the song.

That afternoon I ventured farther afield from the Coş than I had ever been, into a small alley near the center of town where I had been told there

Exam time at the University.

was a copy machine. At the back of the alley was a tiny shop protected by a large metal grill. Inside the shop was a cage and inside the cage a young woman was feeding handwritten lecture notes into a copier. The machine was old and slow. Finally the job was done and the waiting student left. I handed her my song sheet and said *zech* for 'ten', holding up ten fingers. I soon had my ten copies. The price was 150 lei, or about 30 cents. I paid happily and ducked out, savoring my success.

The following week I was prepared for class with photocopies of handwritten exercises in question-asking, and the words to "Blowing." We reviewed the "Wh-" words used in asking questions and each student had a chance to ask 20 questions, of a partner and the class. After a slow start, the questions started flowing and the voices got stronger. I was learning names because all students now had their own handmade namecard in front of them.

The names were new and strange, many of them straight out of my high school Latin textbook: Tiberius, Ovidiu, Caius, Claudiu, Vasile, Ramona, Remus, Romulus. Then some different sounds: Istvan, Ladislaw, Tibor, Atila — for boys with Hungarian backgrounds.

Three times through we sang "Blowin'" along with Peter, Paul and Mary. Only when it was all over did I realize that we had in fact been practicing questions in a new way (how many roads? How many times? How many seas?) The third time around the effect was truly musical, with harmony and gusto, and as I sang, I saw that every student was singing too.

A spirit was building. I was a big hit when I showed them how to make a grilled cheese sandwich, using pantomime and describing the process in easy English. As I packed up at the end of class, three students offered to carry my tape recorder so I was mercifully unencumbered on the 15-minute walk home. Once there, I invited them up to my room. We talked for an hour and everyone left with a reading book. My lending library, which eventually would grow to 85 titles, was open for business. And my friendship with chemistry students Iancu (with the ponytail) and Laci had begun.

—⟋❀⟍—⟋❀⟍—⟋❀⟍

Radu's Defeat

I went to Romania because one man invited me. Radu Vladea, an intellectual and an esteemed professor of chemistry, also held an important position as rector of the technical university where I was now teaching. The preceding year he had been elected to that position by his colleagues in the university. He was also active in opposition politics, travelling throughout the country making speeches against President Iliescu and in support of a new political party, the Democratic Convention. A general election was scheduled for the fall. Most Romanians state flatly that they dislike politics and change the subject. Radu was different. He was not afraid to take a stand for change. He was eloquent and humble, with a warm personality. I had seen that the people who worked with him worshipped him. Someone told me his name had been mentioned as a presidential candidate to run on a reform program against the incumbent, a former communist.

I had been in Romania about six weeks when I opened a newspaper and to my horror saw a headline that said Radu had lost the election for rector by one vote. Shaking, I grabbed my Romanian-English dictionary and translated the rest of the article. Radu charged that the election had been rigged, that the party in power (the National Salvation Front) had organized a campaign of dirty tricks to intimidate him, that his wife and children were being threatened and that the ballot box had been stuffed with illegal ballots. He rejected the intimidation and, in print, appealed the election to the Minister of Education. The newspaper, a liberal voice, said the minister was expected to support him.

I could get no one to talk about what was happening to Radu. It was as if the old communist system was back and the walls had ears. The next day's paper had no story on the election, nor the next or the next. One day I saw Radu's official car, the one I had traveled in from Budapest, in front of the Polytech. Florin, the driver with a cousin in the states, was sitting morosely at the wheel. I walked up to him and asked in Romanian how Mr. Vladea was doing. Drawing a finger across his throat, Florin said, "It's over." It seems the Minister of Education had not supported Radu. Then he said in English, "This is a beautiful man," and put his hand over his heart. He was about to cry.

Radu's fall was bad for Romania and bad for me. He was my sponsor and mentor. He was the reason I had come to Romania and, with the exception of a couple of students, no one else cared whether I stayed or went home. I decided that if I wanted to stay in Timişoara I would have to build some bridges and open some doors. Quickly.

Shall I Stay?

The next day I set up a meeting with Rodica to discuss my classes, summer activities and the following year. I had figured out that the summer was down time as far as teaching goes. Students finished their one-month exam period in mid-July. Then they went on vacation until October 1. What was the point of my being here if there were no students? I would have to create my own teaching program.

I also hoped to find out something about Radu's fall from power but when I mentioned the recent events at our meeting, Rodica said shortly, "Yes, it is unfortunate." No elaboration was forthcoming so I dropped the subject, disappointed.

Breaking an uncomfortable silence, I proposed three things to Rodica: that within the next month I teach a preparation course for the TOEFL exam to teaching assistants; offer an intensive conversation class in July; that she hire me as a regular English teacher for the fall.

The TOEFL (Test of English as a Foreign Language) is the language exam all candidates for fellowships and scholarships in American universities must take to be considered for the highly sought-after programs that include paid teaching jobs as well as individual degree work. I had an excellent TOEFL prep book with tapes that I had bought on a whim the day before I left.

Rodica asked how I would be paid for this work. I had been getting signals from people that no one works for free in Romania; the concept of volunteer work is not only not understood, it is even suspect. I explained that my arrangement with Radu was that payment would be my board and room at the Coş and so while I lived there I should be teaching someone!

Then I asked her directly if she wanted me to teach in her program the following fall. She said yes, if the Ministry agreed. OK, I said, for that I would have to be paid a *lei* salary because I did not want to live in the Coş any longer than necessary. She said she would start the paperwork. Students who were interested in the TOEFL class would have to be interviewed and we agreed to announce the interviews right away. I left the meeting encouraged. It felt as if my instincts were on track.

-6-6-6-

The Warning

At my request, the department secretary posted a notice about interviews for the TOEFL class. Two days later over forty young Polytech teaching assistants, all in their mid- to late-twenties, were waiting for me in the hall. All spoke some English. All were very curious about me. Most had never met an American much less conversed in English for more than two minutes. I conducted five minute interviews with each, making clear that this eight-session class would be "teaching to the test," would be pretty intense with only limited opportunity to speak, and that only thirty could participate. I made the selection decision immediately after each interview. The first class was slated for the following week.

Time to figure out what I'm going to teach the TOEFL students on Wednesday. Probably just go right to the TOEFL textbook... yes, that's what I should do... let me see, it's yellow and black...on the lower shelf with the dictionaries. I really should have a special place for this book because it's so valuable...the tape too.

Oh,oh ......not there...look again....under the bottom shelf with the lesson copies. Not there.

OK. Then it's on the top shelf.

Red and blue spines looking out at me...books I collected so carefully in Washington, packed so tightly in my suitcase and now arranged so nicely by height on the top shelf.... so many green books, red and blue books... but where is the yellow and black one?

Don't panic, Anne, it's got to be here.

I grab my briefcase and dump the contents on the bed. No yellow and black book. No tapes. I drag the chair over to the armoire. Climb up and ransack the top shelves where I keep underwear, scarves and sweaters. Not there. There are no more hiding places in this small room. I open the door to the hall, walk up and down looking for Yoli, the Hungarian chambermaid who likes me. She's three rooms down making a bed.

"Ai văzut pe cineva în camera mea?" (Did you see a person in my room?)

She straightens up, surprised and a little nervous. "Astazi, doamna?" (Today, madam?)

"Poate. Am pierdut o carte. Galbenă." (Maybe. I've lost a book. Yellow)

"Nu. A fost un student ieri." (No. There was a student yesterday)

"Da, ştiu. Nu face nimic. Mulţumesc." (Yes, I know. Never mind. Thank you.)

I return to my room and sit on the bed. My heart is beating too fast.

I cannot teach a TOEFL class without this book. Everyone has signed up. Didn't I tell Rodica about the book? Yes. And she was very interested. She said no one else has such a book in Timişoara. Maybe she bribed her way into my room and took it…to discredit me, make it impossible for me to teach. She clearly doesn't want me to be here. Everyone else has welcomed me but not her. She has that ingratiating smile and that way of never giving me a direct answer. Yes. And I showed her the book day before yesterday.

I look around the room. Where is the microphone hidden? Maybe in that funny hole near the ceiling. Almost every home in Romania used to be bugged. Surely this hotel was bugged, too. They're probably listening right now.

Someone who wants to discredit me entered the room and took the book. It used to happen that way. That's the only explanation.

—◦—◦—◦—

That night I was to meet with two Americans — Tom and Irv — at the Hotel Continental. They were both connected with an adoption/social work agency just setting up in town. I had met them only briefly and we were getting together mainly because we all felt the need to talk candidly about what we were doing and learning. We were just about the only Americans in town.

I was late and agitated when I sat down at the table covered in white linen. Breathlessly, I explained that I thought someone had stolen a valuable book from my room in an effort to discredit me in the eyes of my students. Did that sound crazy? I asked.

"Well, we know that they're listening in on our phone," said Tom. "I can hear them breathing."

"I think there's someone at the Polytech who doesn't want me here," I said unsteadily. "I think they got into my room and took the book to prevent me from teaching a course next week."

The two men looked at me with curiosity and I could tell they were wondering if I was hysterical.

"Well, maybe I'm overreacting. I don't usually do things like this."

They laughed. Tom said, "Never mind. Absolutely anything can happen here. And does."

The subject changed and I did not mention it again. I left after eating only a little of the tasty dinner and returned to my room to take one last look. The book wasn't there.

The next morning I awoke to the screech of the 1920 telephone. Nadina, a student, was downstairs. Could she come up? Of course. A few moments later she knocked softly on my door.

"I just wanted to return this book before my class because you said you needed it this week," she said, handing me a packet.

There they were. The yellow and black book and the cassette tape. I had lent them to her and completely forgotten about it. I thanked Nadina and waved goodbye from my balcony.

Then I sat down and took stock. This was serious. I had created in my mind a scenario of sabotage and vindictiveness and let it consume me to the point of paranoia. Maybe I was beginning to lose my grip on reality. I acknowledged to myself that my situation was unusual and that I could be forgiven for not being entirely rational.

So I forgave myself. But I also acknowledged that this had been a close call, a warning. I was no longer in control of my life. And I had chosen this path. I would have to be more flexible and roll with the punches. Strange, frustrating, unfathomable and annoying things were going to happen all the time and I couldn't let them get to me. In a bad situation I would have to do my best and then just let go.

I remembered a line from Shakespeare, "That way madness lies." No thanks. I would not go mad. I would pay attention to the warning.

—❦—❦—❦—

Friday, June 19, 1992

Dear Dad and Everyone Else,

It has been eight weeks since I arrived in Romania. I look around my small room and see a real home away from home. Map of Eastern Europe. Album of family photos. CD player/tape deck. A neat row of tapes, mostly classical. A row of books on the floor under my table/desk. A bottle of Romanian Merlot, a bottle of mineral water, a jar of Maxwell House Instant. A huge Romanian-English dictionary (a loan), a jar of pencils and pens and the MOMA calendar from my desk at home. Outside on my little balcony are two petunia plants and some bread crumbs for my dove friends. My laundry is drying nicely in the sun. Soon I'll get out my travel steam iron and iron my blouses. Everything is cotton. It's 85 degrees and getting humid.

This is the end of the workweek, and most offices closed up at noon or before. I've already been to the market to buy lettuce, cucumbers, peppers and (surprise) peaches. I also bought chocolate, a small baguette of bread and a litre of kiwi drink. Today my chambermaid, Yoli, hauled a small icebox into my room from another room, so now I can have cold beer and keep vegetables. My room is becoming an oasis.

I've just listened to the BBC news on my Russian-made short -wave radio. You can't imagine what it means to have news in English. I am no longer isolated.

Love, Annie

⚘⚘⚘

The TOEFL Class

At our first meeting, I asked the thirty students if they would be willing to pay for photocopies of the practice tests, at 10 lei per page, for them to use (and keep), since the Polytech was unwilling to foot the bill. Everyone said Yes without reservation. At the next class I provided each student with ten pages. An envelope was passed around for each to put in 100 lei and check their name off a list. At the end of the class I had recouped all my money spent on copying. Rodica had said this system wouldn't work.

By the end of the month, meeting twice a week, all the students had improved their test scores by substantial margins. Several subsequently took the real test in Bucharest and scored well over 600, enough to be accepted at Harvard.

Our last activity together was reading and talking about John F. Kennedy's inaugural address. To end the class, I read his words aloud, over appropriately dramatic music playing on my tape recorder.

While the test results were gratifying, the most important outcome of the class for me personally were the friendships I made with young Romanian professionals. I found them intelligent, hard-working, friendly and eager to learn about the West. They were also desperate for opportunities to speak the language they had spent so many years studying.

On the afternoon of our last class, six of the "boys" invited me for a beer on the terrace of the Continental. We stayed there several hours, enjoying the summer afternoon, the company and the beer. The conversation was lively and wide-ranging: the history of Romania; Greek philosophers; the old requirement of membership in the Communist Party to guarantee advancement at work (most had been members); the upcoming Romanian and American elections; the relative advantages of marriage vs. the single life.

This opportunity to discuss ideas was deeply satisfying to me. I had not realized how deprived I was of intellectual stimulation, how much I missed the give and take of a good discussion. By the end of the evening, we had decided to organize an English-speaking club of which the nucleus would be the TOEFL class.

─◦─◦─◦

Machina Mea ('my car')

One morning in early July in the dining hall for breakfast, I introduced myself to a new English-speaking guest. She was a British woman named Liz, a social worker who had come to Timişoara to work with the orphans, and was closer to my age than anyone else I had met since arriving. She had little of the usual British reserve and we rapidly became friends. And she had something I really envied — a bicycle. A pink one, with 20 speeds. Her first Sunday in town she went for an early morning ride along the river and pronounced it 'grand'. I was jealous.

Because of my arthritic hip, I was getting worn out from walking to distant classrooms lugging my heavy briefcase and two-foot-long tape recorder.

I knew I had to find a way to transport myself and my paraphernalia around town. A car was out. Taxis were an option, but an expensive one. Timişoara's streets were filled with bicyclists, including middle-aged women, some in business clothes. The city was nice and flat with lots of parks and the distances were not great. I decided I wanted a bike.

One day a fellow teacher from the Polytech wheeled up to our classroom building near the railroad station on her bike, looking very jaunty, briefcase strapped into a wire basket. Eagerly I asked her about riding in town. "It's no problem," she said, "if you're careful."

I asked where I could buy a bike and she directed me to the city's one department store. That afternoon I walked to the center and the store, the "Bega" (named after the river that flows through town). They were there, on the third floor, hanging from a long rack. Bicycles — -all the same brand, made in Romania, painted black, one speed, named "Pegas" after the winged horse. At first glance, I thought they were all men's bikes. But looking more closely I saw one lone woman's bike. A disgruntled clerk climbed a ladder and extricated it from the rack. After making sure it was big enough for me, I paid the *lei* price of about $50, and maneuvered it down the stairs to the street.

Fortunately the store was at the edge of a park. I climbed on and after a few wobbly moments was peddling smoothly under the trees. But I was nervous about the streets that were filled with new drivers, aggressive taxis and huge trucks, so I opted for walking the bike the rest of the way home on the sidewalk. I decided to take my time about venturing into the street with my *machina*, which is Romanian for car. Although it was a far cry from my Nova on blocks in Washington, D.C., I finally had wheels.

~~⊚~⊚~⊚~~

Life at the Coş

These were days of intense introspection. I often asked myself how I tolerated the uncertainties of this new life. Planes might or might not fly. Telephones didn't work. Where was my next meal coming from? Could I survive on pork and potatoes? Is this water contaminated? Is my room bugged? Am I lonely? (I had not been lonely since I became a mother 32 years before.)

I was alone much of the time. The advantages of being a pretty young woman were long gone and now I was a middle-aged woman like any other. I didn't have a real friend yet, no one to talk to about little things. No coffees in town to look forward to or chances to unburden myself to someone who cared about me. And no physical closeness. Romanians seemed to like to touch each other so I was hopeful that soon someone would want to touch me.

Helping to keep me centered were the amenities I had brought with me — music tapes and CDs, books, photo album, English teas, a fast diminishing supply of scotch — plus the precious letters from home.

But equally important was my sense of being called to this place to do this work. My spiritual life for two years had been guided by a faith community to which the concept of "call" was central. The Church of the Saviour in Washington encouraged us to listen to our hearts about what direction to steer our lives in, and to respond. Call guided the lives of many in that tiny group, causing them to start projects like affordable housing and job centers for the poor, residential treatment centers, clinics. For me, the sense of being called to this far away place was stronger than earlier calls I had felt to inner city ministry. I had plenty of quiet time to read so I reread a book, *The Company of Strangers*, by Parker Palmer, whom I had heard speak at the church. This time I felt he was speaking directly to me.

Little by little, my brain and body were adapting. My metabolism was slowing down from its Washington peak and I was beginning to derive pleasure from little things…a smile from a gruff hotel staff member; the discovery of a shop which routinely stocked items I wanted; kids playing soccer in a school yard; stray dogs, and babies in prams. The quiet streets and houses near the hotel were becoming familiar. They were becoming my neighborhood.

Returning to the Coş one day I found in my room a new table covered with a snowy white cloth. Some flowers I had received and left in the sink had been placed in a vase and set on the table. It could only have been the chambermaid, Yoli. Because of the small icebox she had procured for my room the week before, I had cold beer, cheese and salami on demand.

Every day Yoli and I greeted each other like long-lost sisters and although our conversations lasted only minutes due to my limited Romanian, we were becoming friends. I showed her my photo album with pictures of my family and home. I learned she had been born in Hungary, married a Romanian, had never had children, and had worked for the last 25 years at the Coş, which under Ceauşescu had been the guest house for visiting communist bosses.

She was never at rest, always bending, pushing, sweeping, scrubbing, or lifting heavy objects while male staff stood and watched. Her smile was warm, her face open, her eyes laughing. Although she was at least 15 years younger than me, we looked the same age. Her life had been much harder than mine; years of physical labor had taken their toll. But unlike me she had no arthritis limp to add years. One afternoon we passed each other on the road on our bikes, baskets full of bread and vegetables. We greeted each other warmly and pedaled on our way. If I had been wearing a headscarf instead of dark glasses, we could both have passed for peasant housewives.

I may have been adjusting to my new home in Room 104, but instinct told me to make a change. Room and board at the Coş were payment for my services as an English teacher, but the man who had arranged this was no longer in charge. If I stayed in Timişoara, it would have to be as a paid teacher. And I would have to find another place to live.

5 A New casa

"Please, teacher. I know a room. It is in the house of my girlfriend's father. When can we go?"

This was Mircea, a tall handsome, neatly dressed chemistry student. I had told my students at our last class that I wanted to move out of the Coş and needed some help in finding a place to live. Mircea and I made a date to see the room the following evening.

By 8:30, Mircea had failed to arrive so I had given up waiting and was getting undressed when the phone rang. "I hope it is not too late," he said from downstairs. Then the standard Romanian excuse, "I had some problems."

"Let's go," I said and threw on some clothes.

We set out on foot across the bridge over the Bega River. It was late June, quite warm and the city lay in a soft lingering twilight. Couples strolled along the riverbank beneath the weeping willows.

We walked down a busy street, trams rumbling past, and stopped in front of a metal gate set in a high crumbling wall. Mircea produced a large brass key and turned it in the lock. The gate opened onto a garden in full bloom—fruit trees, sunflowers, roses, box hedges, cooing doves and a grassy space with lawn chairs. A shaggy sheep dog greeted us, barking and wagging her backside happily. As we rounded the corner of the building I heard loud rock music and laughter. From the garden we stepped down into the basement of a large two-story house. Two tall handsome men in tennis shorts stood drinking beer and smoking. The music was coming from an elaborate stereo system. A colorful pyramid of empty beer cans arranged against the wall decorated the room.

Mircea introduced me as his teacher.

I looked up into the smiling faces of Mihai Coste, father of Mircea's girl-friend Denisa, and his friend "George." George was tall and broad-shouldered and laughed easily. For a moment I thought he was American because he was so relaxed and outgoing. He obviously felt at home with me and spoke English fluently, even to the point of making jokes. In contrast, Mr. Coste was quiet and spoke only Romanian. He had a shock of white hair, a strong nose, blue eyes, a dark suntan, and the legs of an athlete.

The three men guided me into a spacious cool kitchen. I gasped in disbelief. Here was a replica of an American kitchen, with wooden benches along the wall, a table covered with bright oilcloth, lots of counter space and cupboards and two stoves. It was bright and welcoming. I had never seen such a kitchen in Romania. I exclaimed how beautiful it was and said how much I would love to cook in here. Everyone beamed.

The four of us filed up a carved wooden spiral staircase to the first floor of the house. We were in a room with a 20-foot ceiling, a chandelier, oriental carpets, upholstered chairs, carved wooden tables, chairs and desks, a grandfather clock, and shelves lined with books. It reminded me of a turn-of-the-century salon. A large color TV flickered soundlessly. Curved invitingly around the wall in front of the TV was a velours sofa with pillows. Noise from the busy street below was muffled by heavy wooden shutters that had been lowered against the heat.

We passed through French doors to an adjoining bedroom with red plush walls, then into another room with a sofa, carpets and bookshelves. "This would be your room," said Mircea.

I looked at the sofa. "It is also a bed," said George.

"Where would I put all my books?" I asked. George conferred with Mr. Coste who made a gesture of clearing the bookshelves.

"And who sleeps in there?" I asked, indicating the red plush room.

"I do," said Mihai Coste in Romanian. We all laughed.

Then came a moment of great importance. Mr. Coste pointed first to a framed certificate on the wall and then to himself. The document stated that Mihai Coste had participated in the 1964 Olympic games in Tokyo. I turned and looked admiringly at him.

"What sport?" I asked.

"Volley," he said proudly. "I play 25 years volley." And of course that explained all the gorgeous male physiques I was being treated to that afternoon. I was in the presence of some serious athletes.

Back downstairs, preparing to leave, I asked Mr. Coste how much it would cost to rent the room. He looked embarrassed when this was translated, shrugged his shoulders and spread his hands.

I ventured, "Would $70 a month be OK? In dollars?"

"What you like!" he said in English.

I explained I was waiting to hear from the Polytechnic about being hired for the next year and that this would determine whether I stayed in Timişoara.

"I wait you," he said in his deep voice, with a smile and a twinkle. We shook hands. Mircea and I said goodbye and left through the garden gate. Behind us someone turned up the music.

─◎─◎─◎

That night I wrote in my journal, *I think my ship has come in.*

Instinct told me I had to make some inquiries about this family. Why did they have a magnificent house when everyone else lived in small cookie-cutter apartments? Who were these people with whom I would be living in relative intimacy? I closed my eyes and visualized preparing a meal in that kitchen, sitting under the trees in the garden reading a book, seeing friendly faces every day. I decided that job or no job, I would move there...if they checked out.

Since Radu's phone was bugged, he came to my room to talk. After expressing my sadness at his electoral defeat, to which he simply shrugged, I told him about my visit and described the family. He broke into a big grin. "Yes. It's a fine old Timişoara family. Never communist. But I think the wife is no longer there."

"That's right," I said. "She's been gone a year. But there's a sister. And a dog and a cat. And a beautiful garden. Shall I do it?"

"You don't like it here?" he asked looking around the small room. "I see you have made it into a home." He gestured to the rows of books, the flowers, the icebox.

Trying not to offend him, because he had arranged my accommodations, I said, "It's been fine so far. But I can't stay here forever. I want to live in a real home."

He thought for a moment, then said quietly in his deep voice, "Then you should move. It will be OK."

The next day I telephoned Mr. Coste. He was confused. He didn't understand my Romanian or know who I was, until I said *americanca*. Reading from a script provided by Radu, I said I would like to move the following Sunday, one week away.

"*Bine, bine. La revedere.*" Click.

I hung up, not entirely sure I had gotten through to him.

—ⓔ—ⓔ—ⓔ

Saturday, July 4, 1992,
Independence Day

Dear Dad and Everyone Else,

I'm celebrating this day by sitting quietly in my room and thinking about you. I see Kristen in Maine with Becky, Erica and Doug. They're eating lobsters, looking out at the pine woods from the deck and watching the tide come in. Maybe there are some seals popping up in the river. Wherever he is, Will is sleeping. Nick is at a company barbecue in Cleveland. Down in Virginia Beach, Dad is sitting on the porch swing with a friend, sipping a gin and tonic; Barbara is at her home making a cake for two little charges; Ollie is with her boys and their families, and Doris, who is on duty, is making spoonbread for Dad and his date. Up in Boston, Brooke is packing to move to my pad in D.C. In

Pittsburgh, Ned and Trish are making lists of things that haven't been done right in their remodeled house. Morrie is at a fundraising picnic for his boss, the senator. Keith is sailing on Chesapeake Bay. And I am about to go and fix dinner with my English friend Liz who has her very own apartment. We will celebrate independence in all its forms.

After two and a half months, I'm feeling at home and peaceful. My work as an English teacher is enormously rewarding. I'm able to draw on so much of what I have learned in fifty-odd years—humor, acting, literature, different cultures, politics, history, environment, music, art, society's institutions, motherhood. My students now range in age from 19 to 30+. They are starting to trust me and their language skills are improving; we are beginning to have real discussions and an exchange of ideas. I've extended an open invitation to them to visit me when they are in the neighborhood and they are doing so... to borrow a book or just talk.

Love, Annie

First (and last) Bike Hike

When you're in a strange place with no friends, Saturday night is like any other night of the week. But by now, I had a friend, Liz, the English social worker. Her organization had rented her a flat on the other side of town. I was longing to get out of the hotel so I invited myself to dinner at her place and decided to go there on my new bike.

I pedaled slowly through the main streets, just fast enough to stay upright. Clanking trolley buses swerved around me. Bicyclists sped past, glancing back over their shoulders in disbelief.

I arrived safe but trembling at Liz's apartment and it felt great to be in a private home. We celebrated our independence and bizarre situation with a delicious dinner, a bottle of wine followed by *Twin Peaks* (with Romanian subtitles) on one of the two state TV channels. Never mind that I had refused to watch this program at home. It was great to hear English.

The next day was Sunday, a family day when all shops were closed. We decided to take a bike trip out of town since I now also had a bike. Liz had her pink 21-speed touring bike and she went everywhere on it. Our destination was the village of Bazoş, about 20 km outside of town, where there was an arboretum.

In the city, I could keep up with Liz on my monospeed Romanian bike, but once on the open road, she quickly became a pink dot in the distance. Fortunately for my legs there were no hills, but my unfamiliarity with my bike and the road made me unsteady. My legs were getting tired but I kept pumping, counting the red and white roadside kilometer markers. The narrow two-lane road was busy for a Sunday morning and there was a steady stream of large trucks in a hurry to get to Bucharest before nightfall. Tiny Romanian cars and Mercedes sedans with German plates roared past me at 150 km per hour.

At Km 12, I was relieved to find Liz waiting for me. Here we left the main road and headed into the countryside, pedaling leisurely through one village after another. People were enjoying their Sunday and the fine weather. Groups of men in outdoor cafes were drinking beer and plum brandy; women were sitting on benches in front of their houses chatting with each other, their hands busy with needlework or knitting. Children played in the dusty road. Ducks, geese and pigs moved about freely in the ditch. In one village we stopped to watch a mother stork feeding her chicks in their nest atop a telephone pole.

As I pedalled along the peaceful road in the shade of huge poplars, yellow fields of wheat stretching to the purple hills beyond, I remembered my first bicycle trip—in Provence when I was 18. Then, as now, I thought of van Gogh at his easel in the shade of a tree and my pleasure in the pastoral scene was heightened by the memory of those canvases ablaze with primary colors.

After a lunch of fresh bread, cheese, sausage, succulent tomatoes and red wine, we stretched out under a tree and slept. Insects buzzed in the afternoon sun and a gentle breeze bore the earthy smell of barnyards and hayfields. I tried not to think about the ride back to town.

As I feared, it was a nightmare. Not only was the traffic much heavier and more aggressive now, but we were riding into the wind. Night was falling which made it hard to see the potholes. On the outskirts of the city I said goodbye to Liz, and we went our separate ways. My legs were trembling and I had to force myself on each downward thrust. I was scared.

At last I reached my hotel. Wheeling the bike, I staggered through the deserted lobby, through a big door and down some stairs to a dimly lit hallway where I kept the bike. On the last step I stumbled and fell forward onto the cement floor, breaking the fall with my left wrist. As I pulled myself up to a standing position, my wrist started to throb. My left arm dangling by my side, I made my way upstairs in the dark to my room. After holding my wrist for 30 minutes under cold running water, the throbbing lessened. Exhausted and worried, I poured myself a little scotch, put in a Brahms tape and climbed into the narrow bed, ready for sleep. It had been a wonderful but terrifying day, one that I vowed not to repeat.

Two weeks after falling, I presented myself at the orthopedic hospital, in fear and trembling, accompanied by a Romanian teacher. My arm still hurt and was still swollen. An Xray was taken and the woman doctor said I had broken my wrist but that the bones had knitted back together satisfactorily. She gave me an ace bandage to support it and said I should come every day for injections. "Injections of what?" I asked. "An anti-inflammatory," she replied.

With the teacher translating, I explained that I already took such a medication every day for arthritis, and would prefer not to take any more. I thanked her and inquired about payment. There was no charge.

45

(As a result of this accident, my "Romanian wrist" is a bit misshapen but nothing more.)

6 Iancu

During the last weeks of their spring semester, which ended in mid-July, the freshmen in the Chemistry faculty were suddenly given me for a teacher. At that time, they had not had an English teacher since February and neither they nor I knew what to expect. The two boys who had carried my books and tape recorder after our second class were Iancu and Laci (who was Hungarian), and they were best friends. Their English was good and they clearly enjoyed speaking it with me. It was as if a cork had been pulled from a full bottle — all kinds of ideas and questions came tumbling out of them. On that first visit they had stayed for two hours and were the first to borrow books from my little lending library. From them I began to learn about student life in Timişoara.

Iancu, especially, was exhilarated to be speaking English. He would make a statement and then develop it, as in an essay; his command of the language was amazing. With shoulder-length hair that was always stringy and in need of washing, he resembled an unhealthy beatnik. The glasses he wore corrected severe myopia. He had delicate hands with long tapering fingers. His jeans had multiple holes. While he always wore a button on his chest with some outrageous saying in English, he also loved using words of three or more syllables, strings of graphic adjectives and American slang. His one unfortunate characteristic was that he could not look me in the eye but would talk to the wall, the ceiling or the floor.

He quickly discovered he could talk about any subject with me and that I was not easily shocked. He also found I had many strong opinions and frequently became passionate in my conversation. He learned it was OK to disagree with me and did so often.

Iancu was the younger son of a math professor and a Romanian language professor (his father). His older brother was a teaching assistant in computer science. Iancu was a serious student accustomed to receiving top grades. In the eighties, he had been a youth leader in the communist "Young Pioneers." (I think he was nervous about this part of his background, worried that his activism would somehow be held against him after the 1989 "revolution.")

Like most Romanian students, he thrived on American rock music but unlike them, he also read voraciously in English — anything he could get his hands on: history, romance, philosophy, scifi, horror. He was uncomfortable without a book in his hands. His conversation was sprinkled with phrases like "bloody awful," "Gosh," and "Oh, come on!"

One day in early July, Laci knocked softly on my door at the Coş.

He sat silently on my bed, head down, hands clasped between his knees. Then, in a quavering voice, he said, "Anne, a terrible thing happened yesterday. Iancu's mother died. Of a heart attack."

I gasped, knowing that Iancu was very close to his mother.

Laci continued, " It didn't have to happen. She went to the hospital but they didn't diagnose her properly and she died early this morning. It's just so terrible. She didn't have to die. They did nothing for her. We cannot trust our doctors or hospitals. It is a tragedy. This would not have happened in the West. It's so unfair. It's so horrible."

He was fighting back tears and so was I. I put my arm around him and held him. Then we each blew our nose and he told me the details. It was a story of negligence, incompetence and unnecessary death, the first of many horror stories I was to hear about Romanian health care.

For months Iancu wore a black band and was subdued. He didn't open up to me about the loss of his mother but he started coming around more. By then I had moved into Mr. Coste's house and we talked at the kitchen table over tea and homemade cookies. He would sit with hands cupped around his tea enjoying the warmth, eyes downcast, casting an occasional sideways glance at me. Whenever he visited I made sure there was plenty of peanut butter, jam and bread. He would take five minutes covering each slice with the precious stuff and another five to eat it. His capacity for cookies and conversation was infinite. I almost always had to indicate the time to go.

He and his brother were essentially responsible for their family now since their father was unable to cope. Iancu was learning to cook; his brother Horia did the shopping. Although I was never invited to their apartment, I could imagine it: books everywhere, stereo speakers and a tape deck, piles of dirty clothes and audio tapes covering the floor.

47

In our visits I shared many details of my family life and my values, my frustrations with the university system, and classroom anecdotes. He was interested in every aspect of my life, and for me, talking with him was as comforting as a chat with a best friend at home.

He spoke of what it was like to be a student in the new Romania, the many unfair aspects of the system. He was worried about the future, but — unlike most of his contemporaries — Iancu had no desire to leave Romania for the West, a trend we both regretted. He desperately wanted his country to make it in the modern world but had no illusions about how long it would take. He loved the Romanian mountains and valleys and sought wilderness as much as he sought bright lights and live rock. He also loved family life — traditions, celebrations with uncles and cousins in the village — even the convoluted relationships they brought with them.

The following December, when I suddenly decided to go home for Christmas, Iancu seemed worried that I would not come back. To allay his fears, I had him make a list of paperbacks for me to bring back. The morning I left he presented me with a tape he had compiled of his favorite rock pieces. It was entitled, *Away for a Little While.*

7 DON'T WORRY, I'M HAPPY

One afternoon, shortly after I moved into my room in the big house, the phone in the hall rang and I was the only one at home. Quaking, I answered. "*Da?*" I had no idea what the next step was.

The voice on the phone said, "How about dinner tonight?"

My mind raced. Who the heck was this? Probably an American. The voice was familiar. I used to work with it in D.C. Pause.

"Ted?" Ted Achilles had been my boss in Washington and I knew he was now in Bucharest.

He laughed and I was transported back in time and space to the office on K Street.

"Yes, it's me. I'm here with Jill to visit some factories in your town. They gave me your new number at the hotel. Are you free for dinner? If so, tell me when to pick you up and we'll go out on the town."

"First of all," I replied, " 'Dinner' is in the middle of the afternoon, if anyone has thought to prepare it. Sometimes dinner is a banana. So, yes, yes. I would love to go out to a real dinner tonight! Just tell the taxi *Strada Doja 13*, near *Maria* tram stop. They all know it. How about 7?"

"Fine. See you then."

I personally knew of no restaurants in Timişoara. But I had heard about one from a visiting German. He said it was on Strada Mureş and was called "Viorel," which is a Romanian man's first name. Once we were all in the taxi, I explained to the driver what I knew and he nodded knowledgeably.

For nearly thirty minutes we drove around in the suburbs through maze-like neighborhoods of apartment buildings, bumping over potholes and stones in the dirt road. The driver stopped every few blocks to ask a pedestrian if there was a restaurant nearby. Each time, the informant would nod his head and point. Inside the taxi, we were becoming hungry and suspicious as we watched the meter ticking relentlessly. Suddenly, one of us spotted a neon Tuborg sign on a high blank wall. At our command, the driver stopped and jumped out. He returned, smiling broadly, with the news that this was indeed Viorel's Restaurant. Ted paid the fare without an argument. Stepping over rocks and trash, we entered through the stucco wall.

Inside the enclosure was a simple patio with a few plastic chairs and tables. Ted opened the front door and we found ourselves in a spacious room with chandeliers, ornately carved chairs and tables covered with starched white linen. Crystal, silver and fresh flowers graced the tables. After my experience in the Coş dining room, this was an oasis.

A man appeared to welcome us and present us with large ornate menus from which Ted ordered wine and selected several items. After a visit to the kitchen, the waiter informed us that the only available items were sour soup, grilled pork with fried potatoes and chicken — a disappointment but by this time we were enjoying the wine and company too much to care. I had my first green salad in weeks, plus three vegetables, overcooked but full of taste, and Italian ice cream.

Toward the end of our meal, a few other restaurant patrons had arrived. The women were dressed in shiny gaudy dresses, painted nails, high heels and heavy makeup. Their men wore open shirts, baggy pants and several were unshaven. They were enjoying themselves—drinking, smoking, talking loudly—and occasionally glancing over at us with open curiosity.

It was time to go. Ted paid the bill and although I tried discreetly to see how much it was, I couldn't. Being an unsalaried and impecunious teacher and trying to learn from experience, I asked Ted if he thought we had been cheated by the taxi driver.

"Maybe," he said. "But remember, we didn't tell him the address. Also, Romanians can't afford to eat at restaurants so most have no idea of their locations. It's possible he was taking us for a ride, but what the heck, three thousand lei is less than ten dollars!"

Ted had been in Romania a year and was earning an American salary. I deferred to his wisdom and largess.

-⊘-⊘-⊘-

Thursday, July 16, 1992

Dear Dad and Everyone Else:

I want to tell you about the kindness shown me by Romanians. When they visit, it's the custom to bring flowers (it must be an odd number, an even number means death), or a bag of fruit from their garden or a jar of homemade jam. I've been inundated with flowers and fruit almost since my arrival. At my last class with the thirty teaching assistants, the classroom was filled with flowers. Afterward, six of the "boys" took me to the Continental for cold beer. Today, Mihai (my new landlord) brought me a huge succulent peach from his garden.

Then he repaired the flat tire on my bike. People invite me to their homes , including me in their family life, and they drop by for visits. I am accepting this help and friendship with a grateful heart because, in fact, it is what makes my life here rich and happy.

School is officially over until October 1. To stay busy, I offered to teach a test preparation class (for the thirty teaching assistants) and a conversation class. I' ve had very little down time. Which is good.

I've moved to the home of a sort-of family. I have a room in a large house in the center of town owned by Mihai Coste, a 53-year old man, twice married but now separated and the father of a daughter, 24, and a son, 15. These children live else-where. He shares the 100-year old family home with his sister Ileana, a widow in her 50s. Mr. Coste—Mihai—is a mechanical engineer and has worked in the same factory for 30 years. In 1964 he played on the Romanian Olympic volley ball team, of which he is very proud. He's a nice man. His sister teaches Romanian to foreign students.

Also living here is Simona, a pretty 20-year-old woman from Bucharest who works in an ice cream factory and helps in the house.

And there is Adam, an ancient man who sleeps in a small room in the base-ment or in the grass in the garden and eats food from Ileana's table. Every day he hobbles on his stick to the corner shop to buy cigarettes. His only companion is a baby kitten that lives in his lap. I don't know who he is exactly.

One day I asked Ileana about him. She said simply, "Oh, Adam has always lived in the garden."

Although that didn't explain it very well, I was reluctant to pursue it. It is emblematic of my inability to comprehend much of what I am experiencing. I just accept what I see and hear, and await future enlightenment.

There are also Rita, a shaggy shepherd dog, and Bonzo, a Siamese cat.

I have a room with a sofa bed and a desk and exclusive use of a tiny pink bathroom with a telephone shower as part of the sink and a drain in the floor. When I shower, everything gets soaked — walls, toilet—so I keep my towel in a plastic bag. I have the run of the house and garden. I can walk or bike to the university.

I'm getting ready for Kristen's visit. We'll spend a few days in Timişoara, then head for Budapest, about six hours away by train. The following week we'll take another train about 300 km east, to Sighişoara and Sibiu, both medieval

Saxon walled cities, to Braşov in the mountains and then to Cluj, where we'll meet my Romanian friend, Doina Micu and her brother Dorin. From Cluj we'll go in their car to Moldavia where we'll visit 15th century painted Orthodox monasteries. The color on the outside murals has kept its brilliance over the centuries and no one knows why.

It means so much to me that Kristen wants to spend part of her precious summer vacation with me in Romania. I guess her foreign service childhood gave her a taste for adventure and a desire to get off the beaten track. It certainly did for me. I can't wait for the moment she steps out of the Romanian customs. Mihai's friend George will take us in his car to pick her up at the airport.

I'm rejoicing over the news from the Democratic convention. Linda, please send me a tape of Clinton's acceptance speech.

With love, Annie

8 SEIZE THE DAY

Liviu was a handsome olive-skinned engineer and teaching assistant with a shy smile and soft dark eyes. In the TOEFL class he showed an intensity that appealed to me and I soon found out why. He was a budding entrepreneur with a small subcontracting business. He and his partner fabricated ballast for neon lights. They made them on Liviu's balcony and delivered their product every Friday to their customer, a state factory outside the town of Arad, 56km to the north. The delivery was made in a borrowed Dacia which had been gassed up after many hours of waiting in line.* In existence since 1920, the factory produced railroad cars and had a worldwide reputation for excellence. Every week Liviu and his partner delivered about 500 of the little black boxes with wires sticking out, for which they were paid 280 lei apiece.**

Liviu and his partner were legal, registered as a private company , under the impressive name of RomElectric, and were exempt from the onerous

*Gasoline was in very short supply in western Romania. The economic sanctions against Yugoslavia created a flourishing black market traffic into Serbia, depleting the supply for domestic use. The average citizen with a full jerry can in his car could drive the 60km into Yugoslavia and in a few minutes sell it and earn enough money to feed his family for a week.

** At that time (July 1992) the exchange rate was: $1=350 lei.

Romanian Orthodox monastery in Moldavia

Interior of Orthodox church

Kristen and Transylvanian townspeople

Welcoming family members to Romania

Rural hay wagon

Market vendor

Celebration at Casa Coste Mihai Coste at left

Star students (l to r) Laci, Claudiu and Iancu

Wooden church (Maramureş)

Kristen and Anne in Budapest

Mihai Coste and Anne before the party

taxes for one year. This set them apart from many of their compatriots also testing the waters of the fledgling market economy, who were "black," meaning that they conducted their transactions in cash to avoid paying taxes.

One day after the TOEFL class I had expressed interest in visiting a factory. Toward the end of July, the phone rang and it was Liviu inviting me to go along on a delivery, this one to a large factory complex on the outskirts of Timişoara. I jumped at the chance.

We rode out to the factory on the tram where Liviu requisitioned a seat for me from a man. With quiet chivalry he twice assisted elderly women with the high step up from the platform.

After conducting some transactions behind a closed door, Liviu escorted me to the visitor's entrance of the UMT factory. The day was hot and dry and the waiting room was airless. Soon a woman appeared, well-dressed and smiling broadly, and introduced herself in perfect English.

" I am Dana Oprea, marketing manager of UMT. Welcome to our factory."

We shook hands and set out across an empty open space toward a large building. UMT was a large facility, one of the country's most important factories. It made earth-moving equipment for domestic use and export. The compound contained many large buildings and broad manicured gravel walks and I expected to see thousands of workers. But there was no one in sight. It looked like a ghost town.

"How many workers are there?"

"At the moment, about four thousand. But before 1989, there were ten thousand. Because there have not been orders we have had to reduce the number of workers. You see, we must now generate our own orders. Before, everything came from Bucharest. But now…" Dana paused, spreading her hands and shaking her head. "It is very difficult. We have many problems."

"You're responsible for getting those orders, as marketing director?"

"Yes. And I am welding engineer, not trained in marketing! I have this job for three months. There are many problems." She smiled diffidently. "But we must try. We must learn how to sell!"

Liviu and I followed her into a cavernous building.

"Here is the place where we manufacture the cranes which is our main product." I looked up and saw high above us tracks extending the length of the building. A large crane was inching its way along one of the tracks. A slight mist hung below the lofty ceiling and birds were flying around trying to get out.

Here and there down the length of the building, I could see a few workers, dwarfed by the massive machinery they were handling. Dana spoke cordially to one woman wearing a headscarf who was running a large piece of machinery. The worker addressed Dana as *doama director* (madam director), a term of respect. The factory floor was spotless, in fact in the whole building nothing seemed to be out of place. We strolled deeper into the vast chamber, our voices echoing . Most of the huge machines were silent. A few were attended by a lone worker who did not look up.

"How long have you worked here, Dana?"

"More 15 years. I am welding engineer," she repeated. "My husband also works here. He is heat engineer but will become business manager...."

"Have you ever worked anywhere else?" I asked.

"Never. We both started after finish studies at Polytechnic. Under Ceauşescu, government gave every graduate a job somewhere. My husband and I were lucky. Because of our high marks, we were given jobs here in Timişoara. Is...was, very good factory. The best for cranes in Romania. But now.... who knows? We do not know what to expect. There are so few orders. And our salaries do not rise up."

"How many managers are there?" I asked.

"About forty," said Dana

"And do they all speak English?"

"Some...yes, but most are shy. As I was. But I forced myself to try and now I am speaking English almost every day. I must. Is important for job. And is becoming easier."

"Congratulations! You speak extremely well."

Then I threw out an idea that had been germinating in my mind since our arrival. "Would you like me to work with your managers? I'm an English teacher at the Polytechnic. In fact, Liviu is my student. I would be interested in designing an English course for your managers if it is needed."

"That would be very good," said Dana enthusiastically. "We must speak English for our job. I think I could even get general manager to attend. He needs it more than the others!"

55

"I could meet twice a week with a class. All I would require from you would be photocopies of lessons and a way to get to the factory. It is quite far from my house. I don't think I could manage it on my bicycle."

"That is not a problem. Our driver can pick you up and take you home. I shall discuss the matter with Mr. Minea, the general manager. He would like to meet you. We will come to you. What is your program during the week?"

I knew that by program, she meant 'schedule.' "I'm free on Tuesday and Thursday afternoon."

"We will be at your house on Thursday."

I made sure she meant *joi* (Thursday) and not *marți* (Tuesday), a common English mistake for Romanians. We said goodbye at the front office, with promises to work out plans for me to teach English to the managers. This meant that I would have to figure out how to teach English for business, something I had not done for twenty years.

That day, I realized three important things: 1) I would have to create my own projects here in Romania; 2) instinct was to be my guide; and 3) I must seize the day…every day.

9 Tom Jackson's offer

I had met Tom Jackson by chance in June. It was in a bakery in the town center where the bread was tasty and fresh. I was waiting in line when I heard American English being spoken by a short bearded man and his blonde wife. I turned and looked at them closely, assuming they were missionaries. I started a conversation. They were very friendly. They were not missionaries. They were just about the only Americans I had spoken with since my arrival in late April. It was with Tom and his visiting American lecturer, Irv, that I met the night of my "warning."

Now Tom and I were sitting in my room in Casa Coste, in the gathering dusk of a midsummer Timişoara evening sipping the last of my scotch. He had been talking for the last two hours about his success in community development in Ethiopia where he was a Peace Corps volunteer. He explained that usually a Peace Corps Volunteer completes his two years in a country, returns home, and years later learns there is no trace left of his project. The volunteer might be forever changed but the same cannot be said of his village.

This was not true of Tom's project. The village medical clinic and community center he started in Ethiopia still function. Back home in Grand Rapids he continued in this vein, starting a youth counseling clinic that has developed into a community center. He was clearly a visionary. Today his vision was to introduce social work to the people of Timişoara.

He came to Romania in 1991 to open an adoption agency. A "Christian" agency in Grand Rapids had hired him to do this because of the wrenching television coverage of orphaned and abandoned Romanian children in state institutions, a result of Ceauşescu's natalist policies.* Once in Romania, Tom found the adoption scene chaotic. Foreigners were flocking to Romania and buying babies. No one was in charge. The Romanian government finally acted and slammed the door shut, refusing to allow any international adoptions at all.

Despite the frustrations, Tom had uncovered a need that he felt had to be addressed before adoptions could take place. The need was for trained social workers to work with families and with children in institutions. This category of work disappeared under the communists, although it had existed before World War II.

Within the orphanage system, which was vast, peasant women from the villages functioned as nurses. And there were plenty of doctors and of course plenty of bureaucrats in the system. But no one had been trained in or was aware of, the principles of social work. Quite the contrary, said Tom. They were all busy looking out for themselves... and their jobs.

"Does it matter that there are no social workers?" I asked.

"Yes, you bet it does. Because absolutely no one is looking out for the interests of the children." He rubbed his hand through his neatly trimmed salt and pepper beard. "Before we can arrange responsible adoptions, we

*Ceauşescu was convinced that the key to industrial growth lay in building a larger workforce, and as early as 1966 banned abortions and contraception for any married woman under 40 with less than four children (in 1972 the limits were raised to 45 and five). In the 1980s, when developing paranoia and his personality cult put him increasingly out of touch with ordinary people, he introduced the "Baby Police" and compulsory gynecological examinations, to ensure that women were not trying to avoid their "patriotic duty." Many couples were compelled to put children in state orphanages, technically "abandoning" them. Unmarried people and married couples without children were penalized by higher taxes. (from *Romania: the Rough Guide* by Tim Burford and Dan Richardson, Penguin Books, London 1998, page 354)

have to train social workers here in Timişoara, get them placed in local agencies, and show everyone how necessary they are."

Kristen and Romanian orphan

"How are you going to do that?"

"We've already graduated one group of trainees from a ten month course," he said excitedly. "Last year I put together some lectures using Romanian academics — psychologists and sociologists — plus a couple of visiting lecturers like Irv — you met him — and I gave some lectures myself, straight out of my first year MSW survey textbook. But for my lectures, I had to hire a translator to translate everything into Romanian. It took forever. Many of the students are graduate engineers for whom there are no longer any jobs."

He paused and leaned back in my guest chair. "They're very smart but we have to teach them English. So they can understand me and the social work literature. So they can participate in international conferences and communicate with people from all over. Because everything is in English. And it's not just a matter of vocabulary. They don't understand the concepts. They've never had to. Someone has to take the time to explore the concepts with them."

He paused and leaned forward. "I'd like to hire you to teach them. I will pay you $200 a month in dollars. Are you interested?"

"Before I say yes, I'd like to ask a couple of questions about your employer, Tom. First, are they evangelical, and second are they actively anti-choice? Until now I've only worked for organizations whose values are the same as mine."

"Well, no to the first and a half-no to the second. Bethany doesn't proselytize. But it is quite strongly pro-life."

"How strongly? Do they picket abortion clinics? Do they support Operation Rescue?"

"No. But as an adoption agency, they are committed to alternatives to abortion. I hope that isn't a stopper for you. I really need you to do this, Anne."

I looked away. It would mean another activity for me and some real money, both of which I needed badly. It would mean developing a whole new course of English for Social Work. It would involve me in a different segment of society.

"OK, Tom. I'll do it. Thanks for the offer. Let's drink to it!"

By accepting Tom's offer, I added another string to my bow and another reason to stay.

 CLAUDIA

Claudia Popescu was my first Romanian friend. We were both English teachers at the Polytechnic. One day in early summer of 1992, when I had been in Timişoara about two months, we met each other on the bridge that led to the Polytechnic. She wasn't sure of my name and I didn't know hers, only her face. We introduced ourselves and spent the next thirty minutes standing on the bridge comparing teaching notes. This was the first chance I had had to talk with a colleague about work. None of the teachers where I had been teaching since April had made an effort to get to know me, to show me the ropes, or to share. I was surprised at this and disappointed. I had many questions and even more comments on what I had experienced in the last six weeks.

The school year was almost over. Students were already preparing for exams which were given over a period of three weeks. I asked Claudia what she was planning to do during the summer vacation. Not much was her reply; she was looking forward to having lots of time to read. Would she be interested in teaching a conversation class with me? Her eyes lit up and she grinned. "Oh that would be fun! I've always wanted to do something like that." I had struck a chord. Finally.

Unlike most Romanian professional women, Claudia wore no makeup, perhaps because she was no longer trying to attract a man. She was in her mid-thirties, short and slight, with an angular face and dark beady eyes. Her movements were quick and birdlike, and her expressions changed rapidly. Her openness and hearty responses, punctuated by bursts of raucous head-thrown-back laughter, made her a joy to be with. Her serious side emerged when we talked about our students or about Romanian politics — no laughing matters. Her hatred of Iliescu was total, but she saw nothing much better in the opposition.

It wasn't long before I was invited to Claudia's to plan our course. She lived with her aging parents in a three-story apartment building next to the closed synagogue. The 300-year-old building was visibly crumbling, the stone steps leading up from the street gently curved from centuries of footsteps. It was a square building, open in the center, creating a quiet sun-filled atrium with plants and laundry decorating the balcony railings. On each landing a pull-chain toilet served the four apartments on that floor. To save money, Claudia walked across town every day to the university. She rarely rode a tram. She had no telephone.

Her mother, stooped with osteoporosis and arthritis, dressed in a faded housedress and grinning, greeted me with warmth. She was in her mid-seventies but looked a decade older. The presence of an American in her flat was clearly a big event for her. Our first topic of conversation was her various ailments, followed by questions about my family and how I liked Timișoara. Then Claudia dismissed her mother, who shuffled off into the other room of the apartment, and served me lunch: crepes filled with creamed mushrooms and parsley, roast chicken, fresh green peas, cake, and strong coffee in a tiny cup. We finished a bottle of Cabernet Sauvignon from one of the many Romanian vineyards.

The room we sat in faced the street. Through the open windows, framed by gently billowing curtains, came the rumble of trams every few minutes and voices of people on their way to the city's main open air market. Outside it was hot, but in here, protected by walls two feet thick, we were cool. In this room, Claudia slept in a bed that folded up into a cupboard, prepared her lessons and entertained her guests. An elaborate mahogany wall system held her books in three languages. The room was immaculate — no trace of the dust that blew through the city day and night — the dark wood furniture gleaming, the green plants healthy. It was a restful, welcoming place.

Using my few books on teaching English conversation plus some newspaper articles from the NY Times, Claudia and I put together our course. The first class was attended by twelve Polytech students who had just completed a rigorous exam session but came to see what we were about, even though most of their friends were on their way to the mountains or the Black Sea. Claudia and I made clear that the class was to be whatever the students wanted and would be tailored to their needs. At that first class the students decided they would call themselves a "conversation club." This set the tone for a completely different kind of class than they had ever experienced at their university or high school. To begin with, we sat in a circle so that the two teachers were not in positions of authority.

At first it was hard to get conversations going; in fact, it was like pulling teeth. Students clearly did not trust their language skills or their ideas. And

Claudia

Claudia and I spent a lot of time asking questions. We found that the newspaper materials were not working, because the topics — one of which was the Los Angeles race riots — were totally unfamiliar and not of particular interest. So we abandoned most of our lesson plans and listened to students to ascertain what they were interested in.

By the eighth and last class, we had become a cohesive group, involved with each other, eager to share. The students' initial shyness and lack of self-confidence had mostly disappeared and Claudia and I had improved our own skills in leading a conversation class.

On that last day, each student talked about a topic of his/her choosing, answering questions from the others. Examples of the topics: AIDS, living with parents, women engineers and women's rights. In earlier classes we had practiced how to argue and disagree and still be polite. That day there were some lively discussions, causing Claudia and me to feel that they — and we — had learned something new and valuable. At the conclusion, our students, now excited about getting away from school to be with their friends, presented us with a beautiful flower bouquet.

What I learned was that the most important thing I brought to my teaching was my freedom to do things in a new way. I learned that these students needed to develop confidence in their ideas and their language skills. I concluded that the Romanian teachers' practice of correcting a student in mid-sentence stifled the student's spontaneity and created a fear of punishment. I learned that I must never stop listening to my students and reflecting on whether what I was doing with them was helping them to communicate.

But the most wonderful part of our "team teaching" effort was the relationship Claudia and I formed that summer. In the years ahead we would spend hours talking about how to be better teachers and how to deal with the petty bureaucracy problems of the language department. She educated me in the politics of her country, a subject most of my new Romanian friends avoided. She told me her story of being sent, upon graduation from the 'philology' faculty in 1965, to teach in a remote village in eastern Romania. This was during the communist era when every graduate was guaranteed a job but was not allowed to choose the job or the location. Deprived of sufficient money, housing, hot water and food, she spent two years trying to stay healthy while teaching English to the uninterested, hungry children of peasants. Finally, after pulling all the strings she could and paying bribes, she was reassigned to her hometown of Timişoara, and resumed life with her parents.

Our friendship endured for seven years, fostered in part by our standing arrangement to eat Sunday lunch alternately at each other's home. Because she had no phone, this date was hardly ever broken. Even when Claudia was diagnosed with a benign tumor in her uterus which made eating unpleasant and walking painful, we continued to cook for each other. Without children of her own, she took great delight in the news of my children and the photos that documented their progression toward marriage and parenthood.

It was because of friendships like this that I stayed so long.

 SHARING ROMANIA

It was early August and hot. The road in front of the airport building was filled with people awaiting, like us, the arrival of friends and relatives on the weekly Tarom flight from Germany. Mihai, George and I had come to pick up my daughter Kristen who was flying in from Washington, via Frankfurt. No one was allowed inside the building which was occupied by the customs officials so we had to wait outside to catch our first glimpse of the travelers. A chunky square-jawed soldier, rifle strapped to his back, guarded the door. Every few minutes the door opened and a traveler loaded with luggage emerged, looking tired but relieved that the ordeal in customs was over. They were greeted with kisses on both cheeks, exclamations of joy, loaded with their bursting suitcases and plastic bags into tiny Dacias, and driven off.

Each time the door opened we strained for a glimpse of my six-foot blonde blue-eyed daughter, but she didn't appear. The sun beat down on us. No amount of pleading with the soldier to let us inside availed. We had to wait. It had been an hour and a half since the plane landed.

The crowd was thinning as one passenger after another emerged and was welcomed home. I was now really upset, certain that something had gone wrong and Kristen was not on the plane. Suddenly the door opened and there she was, pushing an enormous plastic suitcase, camera and purse slung over her shoulder, a turquoise fanny pack around her middle, huge Nikes on her feet. She saw me and burst into tears.

"Oh my God, mom, you're really here! I thought I would never get out of there! But I made it!"

We hugged each other tightly for a long time. It felt like a homecoming because having her here with my arms around her made it home for me.

She wiped her eyes with a Kleenex and turned to Mihai with her beautiful smile. "You must be Mihai. I'm Kristen."

"Welcome to Timişoara, Kristeen. We are glad you have come." Standing tall, suntanned, Mihai extended his big hand in greeting. She took it, then gave him the first of many hugs of that summer.

George brought his car to the airport door. We loaded the suitcases and then posed in front of the car for a photo of the arrival. As I was returning the camera to its case, a hand gripped my shoulder. I turned around and there was the burly soldier extending his hand for the camera. When I didn't comply, he snatched it from me and started shouting and gesticulating.

Mihai and George listened and then explained to me that it was forbidden to use a camera at the airport, which was a military installation. I understood enough Romanian to know that George then told the soldier that I was an important American teacher and treating me like this would make a very bad impression. But instead of being deterred, the soldier started talking about arresting us. At this point George became heated and shouted that the days of communist bullying were over, that this kind of thing shouldn't happen any more, that no one was doing anything wrong.

I could see that the soldier was not relenting and we had to try to prevent his losing face. Quietly, slowly, I said in Romanian that I was very sorry that I didn't know the rule, that my daughter had just arrived and I was very happy and wanted a little souvenir of the moment. I finished by reaching over and taking the camera from his shoulder, thanked him and turned to get into the car, at which point the soldier threw up his hands in disgust and stomped off. We quickly squeezed into the car and drove out the airport gate. I turned to Kristen who was silent and terrified and said, "Welcome to Romania, sweetie. We won that one."

Kristen was like sunshine. My Romanian friends — who had a tendency toward gloom and depression — seemed to soak up her good health, ebullience, energy and good looks. And she in turn, basked in their welcome and admiration.

A tennis foursome was organized comprising Mihai and Kristen, George and his 17-year old son, Bogdan. They played every afternoon, with great mock rivalry, followed by a swim in the small concrete pool next to the tennis court. We spent many warm evenings next to the pool, drinking beer, laughing and talking.

During the day Kristen and I explored the city, traveling by tram and on foot. Everywhere she attracted attention. She was taller and fairer than most Romanians and her American wardrobe, familiar to most Romanians from TV, drew envious glances. For her part, she was especially drawn to the market where now the stands were laden with abundant fruits and vegetables. The weathered faces of the peasant vendors, the gypsies selling old clothes and the small children hovering around her legs became subjects for her camera.

One day on a tram that was not very crowded, she was set upon by a group of unshaven gypsy men in open shirts who pressed in on her in a group, touching her with their hands. I recognized what was happening and called to her to come with me to the front of the tram. She pushed her way through the men and joined me, shaking. The zipper on her fanny pack had been opened but the camera inside was still there and her money was in my purse. It had been a standard operation by urban thieves who thought she was a tourist and an easy mark. This experience left her frightened and cautious, but it was her only bad memory of Timişoara.

12 Travelers

The Road to Budapest

Only six hours from Timişoara by train, Budapest, Hungary was the place where strung-out Americans living in Timişoara went for R and R*. I had heard stories about the shops there — you could get anything and there were no shortages or lines. Since I had no teaching responsibilities until fall, Kristen and I decided to make a quick trip to Budapest before setting out on our train tour of Transylvania. We bought first class tickets at the downtown rail agency and the next morning rose before dawn and rode the tram the four blocks to the station.

I had never been in a Romanian train station and it was not a pretty sight. The vaulted hall was barely illuminated. A crackling loudspeaker erupted every few minutes. People were milling about, mostly unshaven men in workclothes but also chunky women in drab skirts and headscarves dragging bulging suitcases, plastic bags and food for the journey. I realized with a pang that I had not brought any food or water. The loudspeaker kept blaring urgent information but I could understand not a word. A large overhead board announced arrivals and departures but made no mention of Budapest.

Although I thought we had some time to spare, I was getting nervous. I got in a line and when I reached the agent, asked *"Cind pleaca trenul de Budapest?"* (When does the train for Budapest leave?) *"La şapte."* was the reply. 7 o'clock. 30 minutes away.

"Unde?" "Peron patru."

I said to Kristen, "I think it's platform four."

Then, feeling desperate for some corroboration of the information I pointed to the board and said, *"Unde acolo?"* or, "Where there?"

The agent barked,"Curteech." I stood there, uncomprehending. I had asked about Budapest. What did curteech mean? The people in the line crowded around me, impatient to get at the agent.

"CURTEECH!" she yelled. Then even louder, "...CURTEECH!" as if the louder she yelled the more likely I was to understand. I shrugged my shoulders and moved out of the line to everyone's delight.

Studying the board again I saw several mentions of a place called Curtici. Then I remembered that the last "i" is often dropped in spoken Romanian and the preceding sound is a "ch" sound.

* "R & R" is the acronym for 'rest and recreation', or vacation

So we must be going to Curtici, which when spoken would sound like 'curteech.' We pulled out our map of Romania and found it. Curtici. Right on the border with Hungary. We concluded that only the Romanian destination was announced and anyone going to Budapest would have to go through Curtici.

The train for Curtici was due to arrive in ten minutes on track four. To get there we descended into an underpass and emerged at track four. I stopped a railway employee and pointing to the track number four, asked "Curtici...Budapest?" "*Da, da. Imediat.*" We were OK.

In a few minutes the loudspeaker made three gong-like sounds and barked an unintelligible announcement. We looked to the south. Approaching us slowly in the grey dawn was a huge light, growing steadily larger. Then the clanging of a train bell as a huge engine glided toward us. In awe we regarded the engineer high above us, arm casually draped, cigarette dangling from his mouth. We backed away from the monster and held on to each other.

The first class cars were easy to recognize. Each car had a number written in chalk and we found one to correspond to the pencilled number on the back of our tickets. Edging our bags and bodies through the narrow train corridor we found the seat numbers, piled our possessions onto the overhead racks and settled into the red plush seats. Once upon a time, the car had been luxurious but it was no longer. The floors were spotted, the windows cloudy, the ashtray filled with trash. But the seats were comfortable enough and we discovered they could be extended into a full-length bed, provided no one was sitting in the seat opposite. We shut the door of the compartment, pulled the curtains and prayed no one would join us.

-ⓔ-ⓔ-ⓔ-

Budapest

Descending from the long train ride in the Budapest station, we became part of a youthful throng pressing toward the station entrance, loaded with backpacks, knapsacks, hiking boots, water bottles and funky hats. On every side a different language was being spoken, German, French, Italian, Dutch, English — a river of student tourists heading for Budapest. I wondered if they had all been on our train, perhaps in second class, or if they were disembarking from other trains originating in Western Europe.

Throughout the main part of the imposing station there were helpful signs in several languages — for ticket purchases, information, housing, touring, money changing, even a medical station. Kristen and I headed for a booth that offered accommodation in private homes. The young attendant spoke English and within minutes we had a room in an apartment in the center of town. She also gave us a map of the bus, tram and metro and showed us how to reach the proper street.

The second tram deposited us in a busy intersection, where three avenues came together. We found our avenue and started walking in what we hoped was the right direction. The street was filled with happy well-dressed people who briskly circumvented the temporary roadblock created by the baggage-laden, six-foot-tall female tourists.

Kristen assumed the role of guide/map-reader because I was in a state of shock brought on by the opulence, luxury, colors, noise, and bustling prosperity of Budapest. After only three months in Timişoara, I had begun to feel at home there. Now, in this infinitely more modern and Westernized city I felt as out-of-place as if I had been wearing the headscarf, heavy skirts and stout shoes of a peasant.

The broad sidewalks were lined with stalls filled with consumer goods — brightly colored clothing, cosmetics, drugs, leather goods, paperback books, even pet grooming products. Store windows displayed radios, stereos, TVs, tape decks, electric razors, perfumes, elegant evening dresses, casual Gap-inspired jean sets, leather shoes, childrens' toys, plastic kitchenware...all things one would search for in vain in Timişoara.

Kristen stopped in front of a passageway in one of the old stone buildings with a small blue and white ceramic tile number — 27. But this was a men's and women's clothing store, with expensive items displayed in glass vitrines, not an apartment building. Kris left me standing guard over the luggage while she investigated the passageway. Ten minutes later she emerged, grinning, saying, "OK, Ma. This is it!"

We made our way through the cave-like passage lined with display windows, up some stone stairs gently carved by centuries of footsteps, to the interior of the building and a sunlit atrium. Children were playing there and on the balconies of the eight floors above, laundry was drying in the sun. Here and there a woman leaned on her balcony railing chatting with a neighbor. It was quiet and peaceful, the noise of the big street shut out.

Our room was spacious and consisted of two comfortable single beds, a desk, table and chairs, all in spare Scandinavian style. The owner's books lined the bookshelf — novels in several languages but none in English. Two large French windows reached the ceiling. To get some air I opened one by grasping a large brass handle and guiding the massive structure of glass into the room. An ancient exterior shutter kept the room in darkness, so I raised it by pulling on a frayed cord that fed from a hole in the ceiling. As it clattered upward, sunlight and street noises filled the room. I gazed down, drinking in the busyness, the prosperity, and felt a little thrill of anticipation.

Every one of the handful of Americans in Timişoara had told us we had to visit the Gellert Hotel, swim in the pool there and visit the baths. Neither Kristen nor I had ever been to a "bath" and we weren't sure what to expect. The lobby of the Gellert was filled with Germans and Italians padding around in white terrycloth bathrobes and slippers, sipping wine or coffee or munching on fruit. Soon we too were clothed in terrycloth, our bathing suits underneath. We followed the signs to the 'piscine', accepted the mandatory rubber bathing caps, and eased ourselves into the shimmering green water that flowed from carved lion heads. It was a lovely warm temperature. Floating on my back I could see the sky through a massive glass dome high above and feel the warm sunshine.

The pool was a thing of beauty, designed to look like a Roman bath. It was filled with people of all ages and large enough to accommodate everyone. At the back of the pool chamber was another, smaller pool, waist deep, emitting clouds of steam. Submerging in it was like being in a hot bath at home except that there were many other people in the tub with me, sitting silently on underwater benches. I felt strange and out of place.

But this was nothing compared with what was to come.

Underground corridors led away from the pool to the 'baths'…one for men, one for women. Kristen and I stepped uncertainly through the women's door. We were in another chamber with a high vaulted ceiling and windows that let in the daylight. Clouds of steam rose from two pools. An attendant accepted our token and instructed us to disrobe. Reluctantly we removed our robes and bathing suits. In each pool a dozen or so naked women reclined along the edges. We quickly submerged ourselves and looked around. Most of the women were middle-aged or old. Several clearly suffered from arthritis. I felt an affinity with them since I was similarly afflicted in my hip. After a few minutes in the warm thermal water, I began to relax.

Gradually we began to feel we belonged there and ventured out of our pool into another, and another. We saw that there was a series of pools, showers, douches and water jets, each with a specific mineral content and water temperature, some for specific therapeutic purposes.

After a couple of hours, we had had enough relaxation and nudity and left the baths, even though we were entitled to stay there all afternoon.

We spent the next few days walking around Castle Hill, strolling in the formal gardens, standing with necks craned upward toward the stained glass windows in the cathedral of St. Stephen. We loved the animals of the elaborately sculptured hunt-motif fountain and stood for an hour looking out over the red tiled rooftops of Buda and Pest. We ate our daily meal in small intimate restaurants where Kristen learned to enjoy pork.

One hot afternoon we took a boat to Margit's Island in the middle of the Danube, where we strolled through the park and swam in the biggest pool I've ever seen — at least an acre in size. At night we went to the opera where we heard a mediocre *Don Giovanni* performed in concert with soloists in street clothes standing on the stage in front of an orchestra. We sat near the roof in cheap seats — an orchestra seat would have cost $25. Everyone in the audience appeared to be tourists. The performance was below par so we left at the intermission.

Just as we were beginning to feel at home in the city, having mastered the trams and subway, found congenial restaurants and neighborhood grocery shops, it was time to return to Timişoara. We paid our hostess $45 each in Hungarian currency, thanked her in broken German, and headed for Keleti Pu, the train station. Our bags were stuffed with items for our Romanian household — an electric razor, cosmetics, a plastic tablecloth, kitchen gadgets, and three ice cream scoops for George's ice cream stands. Luckily, we were not hassled by customs at the border and were able to stretch out and sleep undisturbed by other travelers. When the train pulled into Timişoara's Gara de Nord at 2:30am, Mihai and George were there to meet us.

—⚬—⚬—⚬—

Party

Mihai was dubious from the start. He is a shy man, not given to reaching out to strangers.

"A party? Here? Why? Who will come? What will they eat?"

I explained that before we started on our train trip eastward, I wanted Kristen to meet as many of my friends as possible, and that a party was the quickest way to do this. Since it was summer, we could be outside in the garden. That alone would be an incentive to come since everyone I knew lived in a small flat. I said Kristen and I would do all the work. The guests would include students, university people and my friends at the factory, many of whom had already visited me at the house. He reluctantly agreed. Postcards went out to over forty people inviting them to come after 7pm Saturday night to meet my daughter.

We decided we needed three cases of beer — 72 liter bottles. But where did one find cases of beer? It was a commodity always in demand but not always available. Mihai was no help. He had never purchased a case of beer.

The beer factory seemed the best guess but a taxi ride there brought the bad news: no beer that week. Seeing that I was upset, the taxi driver said he knew where we might find beer — in a far suburb. I agreed to be driven there. On the outskirts of town we stopped in front of a hole-in-the-wall shop and the driver hopped out. He returned smiling and beckoned me in. Lining the walls were case after case of premium Timişoara beer. After agreeing on a price for the bottles, the cases and the beer, I paid, the driver hauled the cases to his car and we headed back to town. Everyone was happy. I had beer for the party and the driver had a big tip.

At great expense I purchased 100 paper cups from the supermarket in the town center, plus plastic forks and paper plates. White and red Romanian table wine came from the local grocery. Kristen carried that plus ten two-litre bottles of Coca Cola the short distance to our house. Mihai recommended a bakery in town where he knew the owner, a German, and I ordered a huge supply of salty pastry sticks that I had often eaten at people's homes. These activities were all very time-consuming since we had no car and went everywhere by tram or on foot. The day of the party was approaching and we still had to arrange for food.

We decided to use things that were available locally, not imported. This meant going to the open air market for potatoes and onions (potato salad), eggplant (for cold eggplant salad), sheep cheese (for sandwiches), celery and carrots (for a vegetable plate); to a butcher shop for wurst and other sausages; to a dairy shop for butter. In one exhausting day we managed to buy all the food except the bread and carry it home on the tram in several pungas.

Saturday morning of the party, Kristen went on the bike at 7 to buy fifteen loaves of bread. They didn't all fit into the bike basket and she had to pedal home with a plastic bag over the handlebars. The afternoon was spent chopping, cooking and moving chairs into the garden, while Mihai and his young friend Simona washed and hung curtains, washed windows and scrubbed the kitchen floor. At 5, we all rested awhile, then showered, washed our hair and dressed. By 7 pm, the bar was set up outside to be self-serve, something Mihai disapproved of. The food was arranged buffet-style on the table in the kitchen and music tapes were playing on the stereo. The evening was warm and sultry. The garden looked inviting. Dressed in our best, the four of us awaited our guests.

I had no idea if anyone would come. It was clear that this kind of social event was not what people were used to and as the minutes ticked by, I began to plan what to do with the uneaten food. At 7:45 the gate bell rang. It was three of my Polytech students, almost unrecognizable in their white shirts and pressed trousers, bearing a huge bouquet of lilacs. They seemed intimidated, possibly by the grandeur of the house and garden, but Kristen made them feel at home. Their eyes lit up when they saw the beer supply.

The bell rang again and it was Dana from the factory and her husband, accompanied by the general manager of the factory and his wife. They presented me with two bottles of wine and an armful of roses. Mihai, happy to see someone he knew, greeted them warmly and showed them to some chairs in the garden. The bell rang again. Soon the garden was filled with little groups of people sitting and drinking and smoking.

The head of the university music department, a tall Germanic type, asked for vodka and his wife asked if she could go home and bring back a chair for herself since all the chairs were taken by this time. A happy group of students had occupied the kitchen table to make sandwiches and drink beer. I quickly rescued several plates from the buffet table and gave them to Kristen to pass in the garden. Although people looked as if they were enjoying themselves, there was no movement between groups. Mihai and his friends sat quietly in a row on a bench smoking and drinking and observing the scene. No one was mixing. My foreign service experience came in handy as I realized it was up to Kristen and me to introduce people, move them around and circulate ourselves among the groups.

It was becoming clear to me that parties in Romanian society were different from what I was used to. My guests were not comfortable mixing with people unknown to them, younger or older than them, or not related to them. Since I had never attended a party in Timişoara, I had no idea what to expect. But there were three things that "saved" this party. First, the ample supply of beer; second, the beauty of the evening and the garden; third, the opportunity to converse in English. Most of my guests had never been in a social situation with English-speaking people and for many it was the chance of a lifetime.

People still talk about that party. It seems that what I thought was a near-disaster was an unforgettable event in their lives.

13 ELECTION OF ILIESCU

October 1, 1992

Dear Dad and Everyone Else:

Last Sunday Romanians went to the polls to choose a new president. Two years ago they did the same, and elected Ion Iliescu, the man who had emerged from the chaos of the December '89 "revolution" as the only credible leader in the country. There was little doubt in anyone's mind, then or now, that he remains a communist at heart and rules through the same network of bosses and security police as Ceauşescu. America, the European Community and Western-oriented Romanians have been waiting for the moment when this 'holdover' from communism would be thrown out of office by the forces of democracy.

Well, those forces stumbled last Sunday. THE ROMANIANS HAVE RE-ELECTED ILIESCU in an election that was apparently free and fair. According to a German exit poll, he won about 48% of the vote, while Constantinescu, his democracy-oriented opponent, supported by the U.S. and Germany and the Romanian intelligentsia, won about 33%. Iliescu's support came from the rural areas of the country and from middle-aged and older people.

There are many explanations for the surprise results, but the one most often heard is that the peasants were not won over by the quiet professor (Constantinescu) who preached democracy and market economics, but preferred the familiar Iliescu who did not support radical change. I guess change is scary to people living on the edge. I'm told all the peasants want is bread on the table. Iliescu promised them that and scared them to death about Constantinescu. The last two days of the campaign, Iliescu dropped leaflets from helicopters into the rural areas.

Everyone is saying that it will take more than three years to change the political thinking (they call it "mentality") of people who have lived with communism for fifty years. So the Romanians have rejected the reform candidate...unlike their neighbors the Poles, Czechs, Hungarians, Russians and even the Albanians. It's a bitter pill for the people of Timişoara and Bucharest, who voted overwhelmingly for the loser. I'm as depressed as I will be if the Republicans win in the U.S. next month.

Here on Strada Doja, Mihai is resigned to another four years of hopelessness. Like others, he seems used to bad news. His factory — closed for a month for lack of contracts — will re-open tomorrow, but employees will work only half time and receive only 50% of their salary. On tonight's news we learned that the U.S. Congress, as a result of the election, voted to withhold Most Favored Nation status for Romania. Struggling Romanian businessmen have been patiently waiting for MFN, which was more or less promised if Romania got rid of Iliescu. Even Albania has MFN, and it has one-tenth the intellectual capital and natural resources of Romania! The BBC described the election as "a tragedy for Romania." Several of my new friends have said they are ready to leave.

Autumn is here and I have taken out my woollen clothes. The days are sunny but the nights are getting colder. I sleep in a sweater and socks. Mihai says that hot water for the radiators, which comes from a central power source, will start flowing when there have been three consecutive days of 10 degrees C. The five universities go back into session next Monday. The city is beginning to fill up with students.

Thanks for the red-white-and-blue Clinton/Gore bumper sticker. I put it on my bicycle. I'm feeling wonderful. Very trim because no fast food and lots of walking and bicycling.

To sum up the election, the enclosed local newspaper picture says it all: a small boy draped in an American flag (USA) is planting a kiss on a bored little girl (Romania) with a caption in English, "Goodbye, Romania."

Love, Annie

14 THE FIrsT WINTER

Winter came to Timişoara in late October and hot water started flowing in the radiator pipes in half the city. Our house was in the warm half and we were reasonably comfortable. The streets were filled with hurrying people in heavy grey coats, heads down against the harsh wind. The price of gas doubled and was almost impossible to get. I knew someone who waited in a gas line four days and nights, eating and sleeping in the car, leaving it only to go to the toilet. Trash was piling up because the trash truck had no gas. Gas was being smuggled in huge quantities into Yugoslavia which was under an embargo because of the Bosnian war. Several of my students were smuggling gas. They frequently missed classes and when I questioned them they responded it was a matter of survival, an opportunity to make a lot of money. Embargos and sanctions had no meaning for them.

One day Mihai ceremoniously measured the girth of a large curled-up, fluffed-up ball of fur planted in the window that was Bonzo the Siamese cat, and reported that Bonzo had grown substantially in volume since summer.

The Coste kitchen was always busy then. My housemates, Simona and Ileana, were engaged in what looked like ritualistic preparations for canning fruits. Having grown up in the city, I had never seen this before — the piles of fruit, sacks of sugar, vat-like cooking pots, long rows of jars to be sterilized in the oven, and the final result — rows of sealed jars of compote and jam stored carefully in the pantry, not to be touched without permission from the head of the house. The last evening of the project, we celebrated the completed preparations for winter with small glasses of ţuica, fresh bread and butter and all the peach jam we could eat. I was amazed at the amount of work involved, and also at the fact that the same activity was being pursued in every household I knew of.

I tried to emulate these experienced housekeepers and preserve green beans, which had appeared for only a few short weeks in late summer and were delicious. Following directions in the *Joy of Cooking*, one afternoon I snapped ten kilos of beans, plunged them into boiling water in batches, then in water made cold with precious ice cubes, and finished by storing meal-size quantities of beans in sealed plastic bags I had brought from home. Mihai and the others enjoyed the spectacle of the American with the cookbook in hand making a huge mess. I didn't care because I had been told that the only vegetables in the market in winter would be onions, potatoes and apples, and cabbage in brine. I was already much slimmer than when I had arrived in April and was worried about being the subject of awful jokes about concentration camps when I went home. I had to eat more and better than I had been doing. When winter came, dark and cold, we enjoyed the bright green beans of summer.

My first autumn in Timişoara, I had 18 class hours a week with about 300 different students. My classrooms were scattered all over the city, but depending on the weather and time of day, I could walk, ride my bike or take a tram. One of the buildings I taught in was a huge mausoleum-like place that took up a whole city block and had not seen a repairman since the mid-1930s. In this classroom there was one working fluorescent tube in the ceiling 20 feet up. The blackboard was badly cracked and I usually had to send a student to look for chalk. When it rained, there were pools of water in the dark halls. Windows were broken and often there was no heat. It was a depressing place to teach so I tried to keep things lively and interesting.

There were no textbooks or handouts, unless I photocopied them myself. Students were not accustomed to taking anything home with them, nor were they accustomed to homework. I introduced them to the latter concept with a small measure of success. I found that their professors rarely asked their students' opinions on anything. In my classes, in class discussions and in essays assigned for homework, they were expected to have ideas and to express them.

After these classes, the trip home on my bike through the dark streets was always an adventure, with my briefcase draped over the handlebar and my tape deck in the basket behind. I soon learned the shortcuts and where it was preferable to walk the bike. To indicate my presence in the street, I clutched the handlebars with a flashlight held in one hand. Fortunately, the distances were not great, and at the end of the trip I knew I would find a warm house, music, a glass of wine and friendly faces.

The kitchen was the center of life. Because we had eaten our big meal at 3 pm, evenings were not devoted to eating but to other activities. With the approach of winter it was dark by late afternoon and we instinctively gathered around the kitchen table to talk, keep warm and sip tea or wine. It was at these times that I started teaching Mihai English.

The book I used was well-designed, with small cartoons to illustrate actions and repetitive drills that worked well. The topics centered on activities of daily living. Sometimes we did clapping drills, to practice inflection and emphasis. But Mihai never did manage to pronounce the word "vegetable" as we do, in three syllables. Instead, he would say, "veg-e-tay-bull," since that is the way it is written and it became a family joke. As part of our evening lesson I had many opportunities to point out differences in lifestyle between America and Romania. The American fondness for vegetables was one of them. We laughed a lot.

He was a pretty good student. He never mastered the past tenses but it didn't matter because he became comfortable speaking the language and found he could say almost anything he wanted and be understood. Between lessons he practiced by watching American movies on TV and not looking at the subtitles.

Two evenings a week were devoted to *Dallas* and one to *Twin Peaks*. Mihai, Simona and I would wrap up in quilts and curl up together on the sofa in front of the TV in Mihai's room. This was before the days of cable TV and there were only two government channels. Sometimes we watched Serbian TV because Mihai understood the language.

One evening Mihai appeared in my room with an armful of sticks gathered from the garden. For some reason, the hot water in the radiators had been shut off by the city for two weeks and we were always cold. He opened a little door in the bottom of the ceramic-covered chimney (called a *teracotă*) that stood in the corner of my room, inserted the sticks, lit a match and soon a nice fire was burning. After an hour, my room was toasty from the heat radiating from the tiles. Everyone, including Ileana, came in to sit and talk. We opened a bottle of wine, put an opera on my stereo and talked about the past when the chimney had provided the main source of heat. I learned that their father had been a well-known tenor and their mother an accomplished pianist. During the 1980s, her piano had been sold to buy food.

15 THE FIRST OF MARCH '93

March 19, 1993

Dear Dad and Everyone Else,

The equivalent of Valentine's Day in Romania is March 1, called Mărţişor ('martseeshor'). It is the custom to present girls and women with flowers or a small decoration to wear on the coat. On March 1, I received sixteen little gifts — tiny butterflies, bits of dried flowers and feathers, and other symbols of spring. With them all displayed on my jacket and sweater, I felt like a decorated veteran. They came from my family here, from students and friends. Several people made a special trip to deliver the tiny packets or left them in the mailbox overnight. I was deeply touched. In the recent past, many Valentine's Days have come and gone without any red hearts or cupids to remind me that people care. You see, I'm more sentimental than you suspect!

We had five straight days of snow and now suddenly spring has come. The ice has melted and the hefty women in scarves are sweeping the streets clean. The sun comes up before seven and I no longer have to walk to my 8am class in the dark.

Today I found lettuce, parsley and lemons in the market, as well as the usual potatoes, apples, onions and carrots. But even cabbage has disappeared and the green beans I froze last September are long gone.

Getting enough to eat has been my biggest problem this winter. I'm frequently hungry. I've concluded that Romanians were deprived for so long that they are used to meals of potatoes and gravy, or macaroni, or roast pork. Everyone over 25 has a story of having nothing to eat but potatoes at some time during the Ceauşescu era when food was exported abroad for hard currency but rationed for the citizens.

I've been paying attention to my vitamins and mineral intake. Diet accounts for some of the serious health problems here. And a fifth-year medical student told me that TB, syphilis, pediatric AIDS and trichinosis are very serious problems in Romania. I've also learned from friends about how you get medical care — you bribe the doctor, who is on a small government salary. No bribe, no care. It seems the health care system is very corrupt. Even in medical school, grades can be bought. There are going rates for many courses.

I tell you these things because I think you want to know the truth about life in Romania, not just the quaint, somewhat romanticized impressions I began with eleven months ago. Until now it has been difficult for me, an American, to appreciate what it's like to live without adequate food, health care and good water to drink.

You can probably detect that my life in Timişoara has become normal (to me), and I no longer see things with new eyes. If there is any strangeness left, it has to do with the ability of the human spirit (mine) to survive and thrive under adverse conditions. That is what is happening to me. But what about the Romanians who, unlike me, have few options? Many are depressed, lack hope for the future and seem immobilized. Students, especially, are very pessimistic about their futures. So I seek out and encourage those who are determined to make the most of what they have. My interest is encouragement to keep on.

Thanks to Cathy Bell's shipment of culled paperbacks from her school library, I have a thriving lending library . Most popular titles: 1984 by George Orwell and Hemingway's For Whom the Bell Tolls. And next month I will use Beth Warner's Univ. of Maryland social work texts. Linda's weekly mailing of the NY Times Week in Review is eagerly awaited by me and students.

Love, Annie

16 one year in romania

May 1993. Behind our house the garden was in full bloom — flowering fruit trees, lilac, bluebells, daffodils, forsythia, magnolia and tulips. Ileana bought an umbrella table and four plastic chairs where we sat of a morning or an evening, sipping tea or coffee and listening to the cooing of doves. Although I was learning Romanian quite fast, I had a hard time understanding my housemates' conversations. By now I was an accepted member of the household and if they had something to say to me, they spoke slowly or they spoke in English. It didn't matter to them that I couldn't follow their mundane exchanges; and it didn't matter to me. If I was interested, I watched their body language or asked them to translate. Usually I wasn't interested. It was like attending an opera sung in Italian where the words don't matter; only the costumes, the acting and the music.

Few Romanians had such a garden. Almost everyone lived in apartment blocks. I often wondered how Mihai was allowed to keep his grandfather's house, a dramatic reminder of the way things used to be, before World War

II. I could never bring myself to ask him directly, and concluded it was because he was an Olympian and thus famous. One day he described to me what it had been like there during and after the war. Twenty people lived in the five majestic, high-ceilinged rooms. There was never enough to eat; his mother sold valuable objects to buy food. They ate corn meal and potatoes for breakfast, lunch and dinner. Life was hard, he said, but they always had this beautiful garden and fruit from the one hundred trees planted by Mihai's grandfather.

That year I again celebrated Easter twice. The first Easter was April 11 and I went to the large Baptist church with a student. We couldn't sit together because men and women were separated. The service lasted more than three hours, with two hours devoted to intercessory prayers by women in headscarves begging God to help them in their misfortune. After the Easter lesson came the sacrament of baptism for 55 white-robed adults. The minister stood fully clothed in a pool at the front of the church and dipped each of the 55 completely under water. The congregation of over 1,000 watched intently. I had hoped to hear some traditional Easter music but there was none. The Baptist church in Romania had a lot of American support and money and American clergy came frequently to preach. There was a thriving Sunday School.

The following Sunday was Romanian Orthodox Easter. Just before midnight Saturday, seven of us from Casa Coste walked through the dark streets, across the bridge to the cathedral, the same I had seen on my first night in Romania. Standing on the steps of the cathedral with our candles, we looked out over a sea of people and tiny flickering lights, listened solemnly to a fifteen minute peal of the bells and inhaled the incense that preceded the priests. They arrived, old men with long beards clothed in white and gold with pointed miters on their heads, to process around the church three times. Prayers were sung over a loudspeaker. The inside of the church was filled to overflowing.

Back at the house, we sat around the kitchen table, smoking and nibbling on famous salami from Sibiu, pickled vegetables, cakes, ţuica and beer. The next day, the table decorated elaborately with crystal and china and colored eggs, we feasted on lamb soup, creamed nettles from the garden, roast lamb and potatoes, ice cream and homemade cakes. The wine was a twenty-year old vintage Sauvignon from the Murfartlar region in eastern Romania. As in

Gărînă the year before, we cracked our red eggs together and declared that Christ had risen.

I was not always upbeat. One evening I wrote the following in my journal to dispel feelings of loneliness.

The Stranger is Welcomed When...

The apple vendor greets me with a big smile at the market. We ask about each other's family. He pulls his wife over from the next stall to be introduced.

A colleague invites me to her home for lunch and bakes a tort. Her mother presents me with homemade jam before I leave.

A student with a car, seeing that I walk with difficulty, offers to pick me up every Thursday morning at 7:20 to go to class.

A student invites me and my daughter to stay with her family on our way to Braşov. We spend a day walking up a mountain.

A man on the street asks me for directions to the market.

A group of male teaching assistants, at the close of the TOEFL course, invite me to a café for beer.

A friend writes out the whole story of *Faust* in English before we attend a performance at the opera.

A student invites me to his hometown up north where he spends the weekend showing off his town and we feast on his mother's cooking.

A young student who comes on Sundays for conversation brings a plate of his mother's home-baked cookies every Sunday.

A student escorts me to the beer festival because she knows I won't go alone.

A student invites me to come and press grapes in her father's village.

The ticket seller at the Filharmonica greets me warmly and writes my usual row on the ticket without asking.

My landlord offers to repair my bicycle after I have been hit by another bike. But first he offers me a glass of cognac.

A graduate student presents me with a basket for my new bicycle.

I snuggled down under my covers and fell into a deep sleep.

It's 5:30 Friday evening. The workweek is over and it's time for an event I look forward to every week. I walk out of the gate, down the street toward the river-bank. The willows hang silently over the barely moving water, softly lit by arched lights. It is dusk. Waves of starlings wing noisily over the rooftops to their nightly roosting place. I hear them every evening at this time. I can tell time by them.

Unhurried, I stroll past the crumbling houses, the dark entryways, the once elegant sunken park overgrown with weeds. I cross the bridge and look down at couples strolling along the canal. I'm approaching the town center where taxis wait in a line, their drivers smoking and chatting in the street, periodically pushing their small vehicles forward a few feet. I pass the statue of poet Eminescu and mount the stairs to the Sala Capitol where the Filharmonica Banatul performs every Friday at 6.

Tonight we're going to hear Wagner, Bartok and a Beethoven piano concerto performed by a Korean pianist, Young Hee Song. The 92-piece orchestra will be conducted by Tateo Nakajima, a 25-year old Japanese-Canadian who has come to live in Timişoara with his American wife, an oboist. The lobby of the theater, which doubles as a movie theater the rest of the week, is filled with young people. They are here because of the long-haired young conductor, athletic and handsome, whom they adore.

81

I sit in my usual seat and greet the elderly gentleman who's always there at the end of the row. His clothes are shabby and he is unshaven. I pass him the program which I've just bought for 200 lei. He thanks me, peruses it and gives it back. "Ah, Bartok. Ce frumos! Minunata!" Bartok. How beautiful. Wonderful! He asks me how I am and comments on the weather. Then he turns, as he always does, and begins an animated conversation about music with the older man seated behind him.

A second-year student greets me and introduces her boyfriend. Just as the concertmaster asks the oboe to sound A, my friend Anca slips into the seat next to me. She is a manager at UMT, the factory where I taught, and has come straight from work. Tonight she is dressed stylishly in a cream-colored suit, her shining blonde pageboy and bangs framing her high cheekbones and widely spaced eyes. She looks great. We have attended the concert together every Friday for two years. "Oh good," she says. "Nakajima. I love to watch him. He is so graceful." Last week her favorite bass/baritone, a Timişoara native, was the soloist — her 'boyfriend' as we jokingly called him.

For Anca and me, music is a 'sine qua non' of life, and here in Timişoara there is enough to keep us going. The Filharmonica, founded in 1871, performs weekly from September through May. It has no hall of its own and performs in the movie theater. The opera has twenty productions in its repertoire and has its own hall in the center, with red plush seats, elaborately carved boxes and gilt molding. Although the costumes date from the 40s and the chorus can't act, the singing is marvelous. Two recent productions — Elixir d'Amour and La Traviata — were awarded grants from Western Europe and went on a European tour.

Here at the Filharmonica, the ten or so American and British teachers in Timişoara meet informally at the weekly concerts. We gather at intermission, frequently with guests in tow. We're proud of our philharmonic with its 53 strings, 15 winds, 15 brass, and four percussionists, the muscians elegant in white tie and tails. Such wonderful music is not so accessible to most of us at home. One Peace Corps Volunteer, whose familiarity with classical music was the Lone Ranger theme (William Tell Overture), has begun to develop an appreciation. The other Americans in town are with the evangelical churches. They do not hang out with us; we rarely see them. Many of us are ambivalent about what they're doing here anyway.

Each of us has developed a preference for certain instrumentalists. Mine is the oboist, Laurentiu Baciu, a shy dark-haired man who makes his instrument sing and plays flawlessly with graceful athleticism. He disappeared in midwinter. I learned he had accepted a temporary position with an Italian orchestra which would pay him in hard currency at a rate that was ten times his Romanian salary. He had to leave his wife and child in Timişoara. When he reappeared on the stage in June it was as if an old friend had returned.

Bonds are being forged between me, this orchestra, these people, this city. I am learning their stories. At the same time I am discovering in me a reserve of strength and discipline. I'm learning to live with loneliness. I'm no longer scared of the future, of not knowing what comes next, of not being good enough. Instinct is guiding me. There are no road maps; no rules; no mentors; no certainties. Only the feeling that I belong here.

18 new ways to teach

Social Work

I had been teaching the social work students for four months, since October 1992. They were a group of young people in their twenties, half women, half men, many of them graduate engineers. What little they knew of social work and its basic values had been learned in four months of classes with Tom Jackson and several Romanian teachers. Social work was a new discipline in today's Romania, although it had existed before WWII in a fairly sophisticated form, documented in articles and texts. But these texts were fifty years old and totally out of date. None of these students knew anything about social work as it is understood in the West. They were in this class because they were unemployed and the training offered them at least the possibility of a future job. Victims of Ceaușescu's mania for making Romania into an industrialized state, they had dutifully spent five years in a second-rate engineering program. In 1993, engineers were a dime a dozen. Many were driving taxis.

Our English textbook, of which I had one copy and made photocopies for students, was designed to teach conversational English for everyday living. The exercises worked and the students were beginning to express themselves quite well. But I wanted to introduce them to some social work concepts and get them to begin to use the language in a social work context. In 1993, however, I did not have access to books or the Internet, and since I am not a social worker myself I couldn't create a unit on my own.

Early in January, my sister had sent me a tape of Bill Clinton's acceptance speech at the 1992 Democratic Convention. Listening to the speech in my room on a dark wintry afternoon, I thrilled to the wild applause and cheering, the political rhetoric, and, most of all, Clinton's inspiring words about the kind of society he dreamed of for the United States. I played the tape several times. It occurred to me that these were concepts of a caring society, concepts that my future social workers needed to internalize and work with in their daily activities. I decided to find a way to use the tape in my class.

I borrowed a dual tape recorder to "dub" the one my sister sent and spent an afternoon and an evening deleting the political rhetoric and much of the applause. To my delight, the end product could have been a speech by a theologian or a social worker — exactly what I wanted, and it was much shorter than the original. That weekend I spent the dismal dark days in my room stopping and starting the modified tape and typing the words into my laptop. On Sunday night, by the time the semi-weekly national event *Dallas* was on, I had a twenty minute tape of Clinton orating and a perfectly plausible hard copy. My work done, I could relax, curled up with my housemates on the velours sofa under an ancient quilt, to enjoy the antics of the Ewings.

That week, I introduced a new unit to my social workers, "Qualities of a Caring Society." First we read over the text together, discussing the meaning of words, the concepts, their relevance to Romania. Then we listened to the tape. As Clinton's words rang out in the cavernous classroom, we applauded along with the convention goers. I could see that the adrenaline was surging. At the conclusion, they asked to hear it again.

The next step in the unit was a first for them. They were to write a short essay on "A Quality of a Caring Society," in this case, Romania, choosing a phrase from the speech as inspiration. Following are selections from a few of the essays, with only basic corrections. The ideas and most of the language are original.

"No one is left out, no one is left behind"
(from Clinton's speech)

■ Not all people are born with the gift of adapting in a nonperfect system. Even so, I find this ideal way of putting things very useful, because when we face reality and don't like it, we can try to bring it a little closer to this ideal image. (Stefan Pepelea)

■ We care for each other because we are a big family. We have sisters and brothers, mothers and fathers everywhere. It will be better to leave "our" interests behind and give a helping hand to everyone in need, no matter if they are black or white or red, no matter if they are young or old. Let it be our cause to give everyone a chance to be strong and secure, to never struggle alone in the dark…It is a very happy feeling to be able to look in the eyes of everyone and not feel guilt, indifference, opportunism or forgetfulness. (Mihaela Szappanyos)

■ In the new society he (Clinton) will build, all the people will have a place, their place. It won't matter if they are white or black, man or woman, in good health or with disabilities, rich or poor. They are all human beings, and that's the most important thing, the only thing that matters. People are the same wherever they live. A black mother from Africa, where thousands of children die daily because of hunger and malnutrition, feels the pain the same way a white mother from Romania does whose child dies. (Emilia Mihai)

Child Welfare in a Caring Society

■ In our country, many orphans come from families where they aren't wanted or from families which cannot offer the conditions for a good life. We have to think that children are part of life and we have to do something so where they aren't wanted because families can't care for them, they don't have to be born. One solution is family planning. A social worker can be a good person to help families find the way to have children when they want them…When I speak about orphans, I have in mind Clinton's words: " Don't you ever let anybody tell you you can't become whatever you want to be." (Gaby Curut)

My Vision for Romania

■ The change from a totalitarian system to a democratic one means also a change in the way we think, a change in our value system. Tolerance is something all of us should learn. Tolerance of other people's values, accepting that people can think differently, can and should have different opinions — we don't have to be all of the same opinion. It would lead to a totalitarian system again…A decent standard of living will free us from the daily worries about food, heat, warm water, surviving. We will have time and energy for ourselves and for others, for education, time to reflect…The way for change is open now, even though we don't realize it sometimes. (Sanda Viorel)

■ The Romanian people were a peasant people. They knew how to work the land, and they loved their land. But the communist system spoiled that good organization: it changed the peasants into workers and everything was wrong. Nobody cared for the homeless, the sick, the people with disabilities, or the abandoned children. Caring for people was just a slogan…I hope that people will be changed by us, the social workers. We'll fight for a better life for everybody. (Adelina Fathi)

▍God blessed Romania with rich natural resources. Romanian people were very civilized and welcomed others to come and live here (like Jews, Greeks, Serbs, etc.) Nobody wanted to leave Romania. But when the disaster (communism) began, it couldn't be stopped. Now, after 45 years, people's minds are dominated by total confusion. Under communism, people (most of all children) were confronted with two kinds of truth. One was spoken in society (this truth was not truth but a lie) and the other was spoken in the family, and this was the real truth. Children often didn't understand the difference. About the future, there isn't too much to say because only God knows what will happen.(Roxana Sapuntzis)

These student essays gave me an insight into the recent lives of Romania's youth. I saw them beginning to reflect on the radical changes occurring in their lives now that the dictator had been brought down. I felt their fear of the future but at the same time their hope for a better life. I saw a rebirth of compassion and empathy that had been stifled by a ruthless communist system.

86

—◌—◌—◌

The Circle

Throughout my teaching years in Romania, I was always careful to avoid being openly critical of the system, the methods, the way of doing things. After all, I was a newcomer in so many respects. I sensed from the beginning that many of my teaching colleagues were suspicious of me. Maybe they were also curious about me but they didn't show it. Almost no one wanted to talk with me about teaching methods, curriculum, books, subjects about which I had many, many questions. And from conversations overheard in the teacher's room, I noticed that they didn't talk about these things with each other. Instead, they made coffee together and exchanged stories of "problems" they were having at home or in their social lives. Teachers' meetings were rare and almost always consisted of the department chair laying down the law about administrative matters. We were all on our own when it came to methods and content. I decided that sharing ideas about our work was just not in their tradition.

As I have noted, getting students to speak in English, and to speak their minds, were two of my major goals. One morning before an 8am class, I arrived at school determined to break the mold that day. The ten-minute walk in the cool morning air had cleared my head and allowed a new idea to grow. That idea was to change the configuration of the classroom from rows of desks to a circle.

As the students straggled in, half awake, I set them to moving desks and chairs so that we all sat in a kind of squared off O. In this way, the boys, who always clustered together at the back of the room and contributed little, were all on an equal footing — visually — with the rest of the class. My chair was part of the circle, between two students.

When we were all seated in our new configuration, the students were clearly uncomfortable. Change did not come often in their university life. Predictability was a kind of crutch which absolved them of the obligation to think. Now we were all looking at each other. It was hard to be uninvolved.

I started off that class with a group discussion of something I thought they could all relate to — the TV series *Dallas*. The series was so popular that the twists and turns of the plot were duly reported in the daily paper, sometimes on the front page.

The discussion was a lively one, since the boys were now part of things. The macho character of JR was roundly applauded by the young men. Several spoke about the cars the Ewing brothers drove. The girls talked about the clothes and leisure time activities of the Ewing women. It was a beginning.

In ensuing weeks and months, I sometimes waited until the last 15 minutes of class to create a circle of chairs. (Invariably the cleaning women had restored the desks to their schoolroom format.) At my signal students now eagerly completed the furniture moving and settled themselves. They seemed to look forward to these closing moments. And some were becoming downright voluble. Sometimes I had to resort to calling on the shyer ones. But, unlike their experiences of being called on in other settings, they did not feel I was being punitive or confrontational. Their hesitant comments often showed deep thought processes. The excitement began when students interacted with each other's ideas.

In this way, I came to know many of my students on a deeper level than would have been possible with the standard class format.

Absent informal opportunities to discuss the concept with my colleagues, I prepared the following for an English teachers' conference in 1995. I never received any feedback on it from a teacher.

A Meditation

In a circle there is no back row, front row or teacher's podium. Within the circle you feel invited to communicate with the person across the way. It is OK to quietly observe your neighbor's facial expression and body language. Words hang in the air waiting to be spoken. Dynamic energy waits to be channelled. The circle must be complete, excluding the outside world, forging its components into a unit. I am but one link in the chain; I remind my students they're talking to each other. Today interest in the subject is high. AIDS. There are no downcast eyes or slumping bodies. Not everyone has an opinion and that's OK. The subject is broached and a spark jumps from one student to another as ideas crystallize in individual minds. Some of us are on the edge of our seats. "What did you mean by that, my friend?" asks a student of a colleague. And in responding a student becomes a teacher.

A Matter of Corruption

I did not go to business school. When I graduated from Bryn Mawr in 1956 with a degree in French and English, I went to speedwriting school. This allowed me to get a job in Washington. Most young women my age were secretaries and looking for a husband. I was no exception.

Later, as society and I matured, I read about the rigorous MBA programs at schools such as Harvard, where students get a dose of the real world of business through case studies. When I had been teaching in the Timişoara economics faculty for three years, I decided my students needed something like this and obtained a book of case studies published in Britain for international students. It was perfect.

There were now several other American teachers at the university, teaching economics to volunteer students outside the regular curriculum. I asked them about business case studies. How do they work? How do you teach them? No one could really answer the question. I had to learn by doing.

In the book of case studies, one in particular caught my eye. It was set in Ghana and involved the Ghanian manager of a firm, a subsidiary of a British company. The manager had generated impressive profits despite difficult times. In an audit conducted by a British company, however, it was revealed that the manager had been paying bribes on a large scale to government officials — customs officers, cabinet ministers, and others in authority. The auditors also discovered a serious lack of accountability on the part of the company's financial controller. I saw that this was a case study in corruption. Good.

As I learned from the book's introduction, case studies do not have a right or wrong answer. Students study the facts, identify the core problem, analyze the pros and cons of several courses of action, and decide which is best. It was a great opportunity for my students to work collaboratively in small groups. They would have to wrestle with some real-life business issues that were relevant to Romania. I decided to try it out on a group of seniors, in two consecutive 3-hour classes.

By now I had access to a departmental copier and made enough copies of the case for every two students. First, we read through the case to make sure everyone understood all the elements. Then I divided them into groups of four. (I had found that self-selection resulted in certain groups sticking with each other, namely, boys and the most fluent students, often overwhelming the others.) They were to discuss the case in their groups, following some guidelines from the textbook, reach a consensus (a concept I had to teach them) on how to solve the business problem, and report to the class. 89

I hovered over each group to make sure they were speaking English, and to answer their questions. I could see that the subject interested them but that it was hard for them to stick to English. Usually, but not always, the small group discussions were dominated by one member. I frequently had to intervene to encourage the others to participate and to calm down the talker. Terms such as *accountability*, *bribery* and *bottom line* were explained by me and written on the board. For the first time in their lives, these students were obliged to think as business people, faced with a problem.

It is important to understand that most of these young people had no direct experience with the workings of a market economy. Most of their parents worked for the state. But my students knew that their own futures lay in the private sector, in some kind of business. This is why they had opted to study economics for four years. In their other courses, they were learning a great deal of theory, which most of their teachers gleaned from books. There just wasn't anyone with business experience to teach them. (Until 1990, the economic structure had been centralized, hierarchical, predictable. And corrupt.)

We gathered in our circle to hear the reports from the five small groups. The results:

Group 1: Give the manager a bonus and promote him.

Group 2: Reprimand the manager for paying bribes, but "wink" at the practice.

Group 3: Send the manager to corporate headquarters in England to explain the realities of doing business in West Africa.

Group 4: Fire the manager but give him a big 'severance' check.

Group 5: Demote the manager but allow him to continue doing his job in the old way.

There followed a lively discussion about bribery, profits, and the law. With the exception of two rather quiet students, all believed that the manager was not at fault, that he was doing what was necessary to make a profit for the company, that his actions constituted normal and acceptable business behavior. They were disappointed when they realized there was no "right" answer. This was not what they were used to.

The following day we continued in another mode. We did simulations of conversations among the principals, in Accra and in London. In these little plays, the groups chose one of them to play a principal, and together they outlined what his/her positions should be. Then the actor improvised his dialogue in the simulations to represent the positions. The scenes were extraordinarily good and I began to understand why Romanians are known to be such voluble talkers and tough negotiators. Afterwards, we in the audience commented on their performances.

Next, I had planned to have a debate of opposing views regarding corruption, but it didn't happen. No one wanted to take the anti-corruption position.

At the next class, I took more of a role, presenting a few examples of laws, such as the U.S. Foreign Corrupt Practices Act, that punish corruption. I was obliged to point out that most European countries did not take corruption as seriously as the U.S. "Romania has such a law" was the comment, "but no one pays any attention to it." I gave some examples of American executives who broke our law and are now in jail. In addition, I had collected clippings about corruption from various magazines. In pairs, students were assigned to read a clipping and in the next class, present a summary of its main points. These included World Bank articles on the subject and a description of Transparency International, a fairly new group in Berlin whose mission is to combat corruption in business around the world

One of the most difficult concepts to get across to the students was that corruption has a terrible impact on economic growth. Since economic growth had stalled in Romania and would surely affect their chances for a good life, I thought they might begin to see things a little differently. They did understand the concept of the *level playing field*. When I asked them if they wanted to defend a soccer goal that lay at the bottom of a hill, they saw that a culture of bribes destroys the level playing field of business. I asked the students if their economics professors ever discussed the role of bribery in contemporary Romanian business. The answer was: No, not one.

So I learned about corruption from my students. I learned that it is a way of life for them. I saw that it reached every level of life in Romania, from the bribes paid to ticket agents to get a train home, to gifts to dorm managers for a good room, and worst, of all, to professors for marks. A recent example: In an effort to raise the grade on a poor diploma paper, a student gave his professor 15 kg of fish, a bottle of whiskey and agreed to drive the professor to a distant city.

91

I have no doubt that this culture of corruption, in Romanian *pila* and *relatie*, is one of the reasons investors are staying away. Although politicians pledge to do something about it, the people don't believe them, and they are right. Everyone continues living their lives in the same old way. I like to think that my students now know there is another way, that although corruption is present everywhere, in the most prosperous economies, it is not tolerated.

Most of my students will not become activists. But it is up to them, and their generation, to change things. This is what I told them.

19 A NEW FRIEND

CATALIN (1995)

It's a warm day in spring and I'm sitting under an umbrella advertising Coca Cola in a country café. It's midday and my companions are a handsome muscular man of about 40 and his nine year old daughter. I forget the pain and awkwardness of moving around and am thoroughly enjoying myself. The warm sun makes my senses come alive as does my male companion who laughs a lot, is highly animated and relishing my company. I can feel my taut muscles letting go and the frown lines in my forehead dissolving. Unconsciously I evaluate how I am feeling, and blurt out to Catalin, "I feel absolutely wonderful!" This pleases him.

We settle gratefully in the shade of the red and white umbrella, protected from the noonday sun. Flowering shrubs lining the neat gravel driveway move gently in the breeze. Two ice cold bottles of German beer are placed on the table, two glasses, and a bottle of Coke. Catalin is tanned and handsome and staring intently at me. The young girl skips away with her coke. Her father and I relish the cold beer, the warmth of summer, the privacy of a country café.

For the first time in months my muscles are relaxed and I do not think about how I will maneuver from one spot to the next. The cane is out of sight. Suddenly the man bursts out, "You are so naive, Annie. Do you really think the Securitate does not know about you? Why, your own room probably has at least two microphones and Mihai is making a regular report on you. That is sure. I know. I used to install those microphones. And I saw all those little reports your present boss used to make about the Americans on his staff. What do you think? That this is democracy here? You are wrong."

If I am wrong, I don't care. I'm savouring this moment of pleasure and harmless intimacy with an admiring man. This charming taxi driver and former Securitate officer has befriended me, offered to become my "legs" and sensed my thirst for living. I seem to provide him some kind of excitement — just by being an American. As for me, well, he makes me feel attractive. With him I am released from the arthritis and being nearly sixty years old.

⟨୧⟨୧⟨୧

Many of the taxi drivers in Timişoara were graduate engineers. The dictator Ceauşescu, in his drive to industrialize this agrarian nation, built factories in remote rural areas and poured money into the engineering schools. Upon graduation from university, a student was assigned to one of these factories, based on his or her class standing. Because factories were where the jobs were, high school graduates went into the engineering schools in huge numbers. But after the 'revolution' of 1989, the flow of orders and supplies from the central government to the factories dried up and workers were laid off in the thousands. Since there were no jobs anywhere, men resorted to earning a living driving taxis.

Even though they were cheap, I usually didn't take taxis. But getting home from the market with pungas loaded with fruits and vegetables was awkward and fairly painful (because of my arthritic hips). I started taking taxis. Often the driver was an engineer and enjoyed a chance to practice his English.

One Saturday morning in April 1995, I randomly chose a taxi from the line near the market — like most taxis, a small beat-up four cylinder Dacia. As usual, I loaded my pungas into the back seat and climbed into the front. The driver said in English, "Where are you going?" and I responded in Romanian, "*strada Doja 13.*" Instead of starting the car, he turned to me and said, "My God, you're an American! Who are you? What are you doing here?" I told him I was a teacher at the university. "And what do you think of Romania?" This was a normal question to which I responded automatically, at the same time noticing that he was handsome with an open face and was smiling at me as if I were some kind of movie star. He had not yet started the car.

"What is your name?"

"Anne."

"Well, Annie, I am Catalin. And I love Americans. From today I will be your personal chauffeur!"

And he started the car.

For the next two months, if I needed to call a taxi — and I often did because of the increasing pain in my hips — I would call Catalin's company and ask for his taxi number. All the taxis had radio communication with their dispatcher and within ten minutes, he would be there. If my trip was to the market, he would follow me with the pungas. It made shopping for food a pleasure. Sometimes we drove out to the suburbs and drank a coffee or a beer. Sometimes at midday we went to pick up his daughter at her German school. Like many Romanian families, Catalin and his wife had only one child, although they would have liked a larger family. His wife was a medical school graduate and had a good job representing a French pharmaceutical firm. Catalin had been driving a taxi for several years, unable to find any other job that paid a decent wage. He worked long days and nights but rarely joined the row of empty taxis waiting in line for customers in the city center. Instead, he learned where large meetings or events were being held and went there to offer his personalized services to foreigners.

After graduating from engineering school, Catalin had joined the *Securitate*, Ceauşescu's secret police. One of his jobs had been to plant listening devices in the apartment of the university's Fulbright lecturer. (Perhaps this was a fabrication, but he was able to describe the apartment in some detail.) He lost his job when, assigned to counterintelligence, he uncovered and exposed the corrupt activities of a high-ranking *Securitate* officer who was selling information to the French. The officer was never prosecuted. Catalin said that officer now ran a profitable, formerly state-owned company and had become very rich. He drove me past the apartment house in the center where he lived in luxury.

Hearing these stories from Catalin, even though I assumed they were embellished, helped me understand and appreciate what it had been like to live in a repressive society where every individual had to concentrate on survival and lived in fear of being exposed or denounced. It also helped me understand the anger and frustration I had sensed in many of my friends at their low standard of living and the all-too-visible luxury enjoyed by former communists.

For all his good humor and love of fun, Catalin was an angry man. He seemed to have lost any love of country he may have had and spoke disparagingly of all politicians. He adored his wife and ten-year old daughter and longed for a better life for the three of them. I provided a sounding board for his frustrations. Also, he could tell me almost anything, knowing I would be unable to verify it.

For my part, I was grateful for the male companionship and the boost he gave to my mobility. Those hips were finally getting to me and I was glad I had scheduled joint replacement surgery in Norfolk, Virginia that summer.

20 EPILOGUE

After one full year at the Polytechnic (1992-1993), I moved to another state university, the University of Timişoara. Without Radu Vladea to run interference for me at the Polytechnic, it had been difficult to do a good job. In 1994, to my regret, Radu and his family emigrated to Canada, leaving me 100% on my own.

At the new university, I was befriended by a senior English professor, Tudor Beşuan. He was starting a new department of modern languages within the faculty of Economics and was eager to get me in his program. So I moved in the fall of 1993 and began teaching General English and Business English, mostly to students majoring in International Trade. My salary was the same as a Romanian lecturer, about $100 a month.

At the end of 1994, the arthritis in my hips had worsened and I could no longer ride my bike or walk more than a short distance, so in July 1995 in Norfolk, Virginia, I underwent the first of two total hip replacement operations. During the recuperation period I lived with my father and his caregivers at the beach. A close friend, a retired Marine Corps colonel, took my place at the university in Timişoara for that fall semester. He employed some creative teaching methods. His students still talk about the simulated trial they put on under his tutelage — an experiential lesson in justice and democracy.

I returned to Timişoara eight months later with two nicely working titanium hips. It was time to leave my Romanian family and live on my own. I had a good working knowledge of Romanian, friends all over town, and by then shortages were rare. I found a two-room apartment near the university for $100 a month. Most importantly, I acquired a second-hand 486 laptop which a former student, now a manager in a government communications ministry, prepared for email. An external modem and an account with the city's first ISP, put me in daily touch with the world. Right in my own living room, this miracle of modern telecommunications made up for any remaining inconveniences of living in Central Europe.

When in 1999 I left for good, the graduating classes of 1998 and 1999 at Timişoara U. had had me as their English teacher for four years and we had come to know each other well. I introduced them to many new things, including business case studies, job interviewing techniques, and American slang. I attended their student parties where we danced in dimly lit-halls to ear-splitting disco. They visited me in my apartment for tea. I helped them with scholarship applications and prepped them for interviews. When I left, my suitcases held gifts of delicate *macramé* doilies made by students' grandmothers. I knew that for many of these young people I had been a significant part of their formative years.

I shared this country with others. My daughter made two summer visits before she left for her own adventure in Brazil. At different times, college classmates and their husbands joined me and Tibi (short for Tiberius), a Hungarian friend who loved to drive, on road trips through Transylvania, Bucovina and Maramureş. Our accommodations were always simple: no-star hotels in the cities, the urban apartment of a retired math professor, a wooden house in a tiny mountain village where life has not changed much since the 1800s. Once I calculated what it cost one of these couples to tour with me for ten days in Romania — about $700. They said it was more fun than professionally managed tours to other exotic places for ten times the price. In all, I was able to accompany eight groups of family and friends on trips around Romania.

In her book, *I Dreamed of Africa*, Kuki Gallman quotes something her father said to her when she was a child. "The most important thing you can ever learn in life," he said, "…is to be able to be alone. Sooner or later the time will come when you will be alone with yourself. You must be able to cope and face your own company." (p. 243)

Reading these words a year after I left Romania, I realized they apply to me. I learned to be alone then and to enjoy my own company. Most of the time I was happy and productive, with a sense of purpose. But being alone forced me to reach out to people as I had never done before. The result was lasting friendships with people of all ages that sustained me then, and still do today.

-ⓒ-ⓒ-ⓒ

'Back for a Little While'

During my years of teaching abroad, I returned to America for vacations and hip surgery. But while in the U.S. I was always thinking about my life in Romania: How could I improve my teaching? What materials could I gather to take back with me? What classical CDs would I enjoy most? What music would my students enjoy? I spent hours in bookstores and second-hand shops and the culling shelves of public libraries looking for books to put in my suitcase. The faces of students filled my dreams and waking hours. There was a constant drag, like a rip current, pulling me back to Romania. To be honest, there were things about my home country I could not tolerate — the overabundance, the constant barrage of advertising, the emphasis on consumption. It felt like America was awash in money. When I was at home, my friends were frequently too busy to spend time with me. All was in sharp contrast to my simple life in Romania. I was always eager to return.

In May 2000, ten months after I returned home for good and using frequent flyer miles, I went back for a short visit. Thanks to email, I had been in regular touch with friends and former students and I was longing to see them again.

—๏—๏—๏—

A Cell Phone for Claudia (May 2000)

Monday. *Claudia and I greet each other like long-lost sisters. But she looks terrible. She is gaunt, with circles under her eyes. She says once a month her legs swell up so much she cannot walk. The tumor is growing daily, it seems. She has decided to face reality and see a surgeon. Her mother shuffles in to see me. Her arthritis is so bad she hauls herself around with a broom; suddenly last week, she lost all her hearing. The doctor thinks it's a virus, but she won't go to his office. I leave the quiet apartment with an uneasy feeling.*

Thursday. *Claudia and I meet for lunch in town. The surgeon has been seen and has insisted that Claudia be operated on immediately. The tumor is pressing on vital organs.*

Saturday. *It's two days before I leave and I'm doing some last minute shopping. I pass by the green and white display of a popular cell phone dealer. The door is open. I go in and look at the different models. There is one for about $100. I have much more than that left in the cash I brought with me. In ten minutes I'm out of there with a cell phone for Claudia. Her apartment is ten minutes' walk away. She is at home, with a student. Wordlessly, I give her the bag and a hug, and leave.*

Thursday. *Now I'm back in Washington. I call the cell phone number. Claudia answers. She is lying in a hospital bed, the phone by her side. The day before they removed a 5 kg tumor from her uterus. She says she already feels better.*

Thursday. *It has been two weeks since my last phone call. Claudia answers. She is at home and feeling better than she has in years. She has returned to her classes, part time. Her voice sounds as it did in earlier years. My heart is full.*

—๏—๏—๏—

Babies

On my return visit in 2000, I spent time with a lot of babies. Mihai Coste, my landlord, is now married to a lovely younger woman who presented him with his third child, a daughter, Cristina. After a two-year maternity leave, Mihai's wife returned to her factory job and Mihai, now retired from his factory, has assumed full-time care of Cristina. He loves it when people on the street think she's his granddaughter (he's 60). Sometimes I think that Mihai is the most contented man in Romania.

Claudiu, who had introduced me to several girlfriends over the years, and who set up my email, is a successful businessman and has a son with his doctor wife, another Cristina. And Iancu, who lost both parents in a year, is now a happily married family man with two daughters and a son. But although he and his wife both have jobs and have found what they call a "rent-a-granny," sometimes there is not enough money for even the basics, like Pampers or milk.

Progress

Back in 1992, my first days in Romania were spent in the deserted Saxon mountain village of Garânã which left me with a lasting impression of deterioration and decay. A recent email from a former student described that village today: "…it is so lively. Last summer I went there with my girlfriend to a German festival with traditional folk costumes. There was also a big jazz concert and a summer camp for young sculptors." Perhaps this is a sign.

Politics

In 1996, Romania elected Emil Constantinescu president. A quiet, unassuming professor, he is an intellectual, not a politician. On television he came across as genuine, in contrast to his opponent, Ion Iliescu, an astute politician known for his unctuous smile. Iliescu, a former communist, had been in power since 1990 and had come close to destroying the economy through his reluctance to initiate critical reforms and because of the rampant corruption. As before, Constantinescu had the overt support of the European Union and the U.S.

When Constantinescu was elected, I shared in the euphoria and optimism that pervaded the country. At last Romania was going to join its neighbors to the north in a long- awaited prosperity.

They are still waiting.

Under the new president and his centrist coalition, some economic indicators went up but most continued in a downward spiral and foreign investment dwindled to a trickle. 'Shock therapy' was introduced, with some privatization and budget cuts in state spending. The rate of inflation was reduced, but average Romanians were saddled with huge increases in utility, food and transportation costs while their salary increases were tiny. Thousands lost their jobs. Urban vegetable gardens began to appear in vacant lots. At the same time, the number of cars in the cities increased, creating traffic jams and pollution and many were expensive. (In 1992 when I arrived, most Romanians did not own a car.) Someone is getting rich.

In May 2000 on my short visit, I found people depressed, disappointed with their leaders, more resigned than ever to corruption as a fact of life. As living standards edge toward those of India or Africa, 40 percent of the population lives on less than $35 a month and between 25 and 40 percent of the economy goes untaxed (see NY Times 11-26-00-article by Donald McNeil, Jr). Astonishingly, Mr. Iliescu, the former president who had lost the 1996 election, was running again and seemed ready to win in the fall. In a surprise move, in July 2000, President Constantinescu said he would not run again; polls indicated he and his party faced sure defeat. He blamed corruption, saying, "If we continue to break laws and if theft, crime and lies continue to proliferate, then any investments or support through international programs are in vain."

Into this dispirited scene stepped Corneliu Vadim Tudor, an ultra-right wing nationalist who is president of the Greater Romania Party. In a whirlwind media blitz preceding the November 2000 election, he capitalized on the widespread discontent by blaming minorities for the country's ills and promising to re-nationalize resources and subsidize agriculture — a return to the old days. In the first round of voting (in which there were 13 candidates), he won a stunning 27 percent of the vote, just 11 points behind Iliescu. In the runoff election in December, when a current joke had voters choosing between cancer and AIDS, Iliescu won handily. But the potential for an extremist taking power in the heart of Europe had attracted the world's attention .

—◦—◦—◦—

The Bottom Line — a Job

Despite the poor economy, good private sector jobs are being created and my students are getting some of them. Marius is a management consultant with KPMG, Bogdan and Robert with Price Waterhouse. Cristi works for an American mutinational, Solectron. Cosmin ('98) has already worked for two of the big five American auditing firms. Five in the Class of 2000 have internships in Britain. Cristian has started a career in sales. Dacian is in the international department of a multinational bank in Bucharest. Laci works in marketing in a hot computer game company in Budapest. Remus (Polytech '94) designs software. Mircea is a manager for Philip Morris. Iancu is a chemist for an herbal medicine enterprise.

Many of the social workers who risked studying a new discipline are employed by the state, or by foreign charities working in Romania. Many must work two jobs because the salaries are so low. And of course, many of my students have come to the U.S. or Canada.

All of them use English in their jobs.

While I lived and worked in Timişoara, the world around us was changing rapidly. In a small way I was able to introduce my students to the future that was waiting for them.

It was the greatest privilege accorded me in my life.

—◦—◦—◦—

To Romania with Love

When I sip a thimbleful of your ţuica, fiery and pungent, I hear the tolling of the cathedral bell in Timişoara's Opera Square. I see the cloud of pink cherry blossoms in spring on Bulevard Parvan. I long to rest my eyes on the rolling hills and snow-covered peaks of your Transylvania, on the many hues of green in your fertile valleys.

I miss the rich chords and basso profundo tones of your liturgical music. I miss leisurely sharing strong coffee in tiny cups with friends. I miss the eager faces of my freshman students who had never seen an American.

I ask myself, will I ever again experience anything like the moment I watched horses and cows moving slowly downhill past me in a village in far Maramureş, each animal entering, unattended, its own farmyard gate? In my land of abundance, will I remember the abundance of a traditional Romanian holiday meal, with its many dishes and fleeting sensation of plenty?

Finally, Romania, will I ever forget the words of a student as he handed me a flower at graduation,

"Thank you for coming to us"?

Never.

FIN

APPENDIX I—TIMIŞOARA

Timişoara (pronounced Tim-i-schwa-ra), a city of 325,000 people, is one of the main economic, scientific and cultural centers in Romania. It lies in a rich plain in the western part of the country, very near the border with Serbia/Yugoslavia and six hours by train from Budapest, Hungary. Once a medieval city surrounded by outer walls, it was sacked in the 13th century by the Tartars, rebuilt by Iancu of Hunedoara, and in 1522 captured by the Turks. In 1716 the Hapsburgs claimed the city for the Austro-Hungarian empire where they ruled benignly for two hundred years.

Timişoara is now best known for being the birthplace of the 1989 revolution. It was here that Lazlo Tokes, the dissident Hungarian priest threatened by the local communists with internal exile, refused to leave his church ('Reformed' or Calvinist). Protests at his banishment began on 15 December 1989. The army and police fired on demonstrators for three days, killing 97 people, but their numbers continued to swell. By Dec. 20, 100,000 Timişoarans of all religious beliefs were demonstrating in the city in support of the Hungarian pastor and against the communists. Gradually, troops stopped firing, put down their rifles and joined the students and citizens in the crowd.

In Bucharest, where the dictator Ceauşescu was making a speech, the crowd began chanting "Ti-mi-şoar-a" (it sounded like „tee-mee-schwa-ra") in support of the protestors to the north, an unheard-of act of defiance. The army fired on the growing crowds and many were killed. News spread to other cities and the revolution was in full swing. As in Timişoara, the government troops changed sides, leaving the hated dictator and his wife on their own. The pair tried to flee but were stopped, arrested, tried and executed on Dec. 25, 1989.

Today the city center is a busy pedestrian mall, with shops, cafés, flower and book stalls, surrounded by gingerbread Austro-Hungarian facades. It is always crowded with people out for a walk, window shopping, enjoying ice cream and popcorn. Separating the two sides of the mall is a well-tended garden with benches for older people, a fountain, and an imposing sculpture of Romulus and Remus with their wolf-mother. Pensioners gather in clusters to fulminate, argue, gossip and smoke. At one end of the mall is the Romanian Orthodox Cathedral; at the other the opera house. The *centru* is the pride of the city.

On the city's outskirts new glass and steel 15-story office buildings are being erected next to rusting hulks of unfinished "blocks" from the communist era. Most Timişoarans live in apartment blocks in these suburbs which are devoid of beauty or comfort. The apartments are small and one-size-fits-all.

The city is served by aging trams and buses and competing fleets of inexpensive metered taxis. There are many open air markets where most people buy their fruits and vegetables and where you can also find used clothing, bicycle tires, small paper bags of medicinal herbs, live ducks and chickens, lambs at Easter, and flowers. In every neighborhood there is a pump that brings pure spring water to the surface. Residents who do not trust the city water, which comes from the river, line up with their plastic bottles to pump drinking water for their homes. I had a ten-litre plastic container that I transported on the back of my bike. In the old city there is a quiet well-tended park around every corner. Timişoara is known to Romanians as the City of Flowers.

For comprehensive geographical, historical, political and economic information on Romania, visit The World Factbook website: *www.odci.gov/cia/publications/factbook.* Click "country listing," then "R," then Romania.

Timişoara centru *and Orthodox cathedral*

APPENDIX II — GYPSIES

Descendants of the ancient warrior classes of Northern India (Punjab), gypsies or *Roma* as they prefer to be called, migrated west from the 14th century onward, probably fleeing the advance of Islam. Gradually they became scattered throughout Europe, particularly in Eastern and Central Europe, where they pursued their traditional occupations of blacksmith, cobbler, tinker, horsedealer, toolmaker and performer, especially in music. They came to be called gypsies because people mistakenly thought they came from Egypt.

In the principalities of Wallachia and Moldavia (later Romania), gypsies were slaves, bought and sold by large estate holders and monasteries, until 1864, when the newly-formed nation emancipated them. Today there are about 3.5 million gypsies in Romania, ten million in the region east of Vienna. Nearly all are settled, no longer nomadic.

A 1993 New York Times article had this to say about gypsies and the new freedom from communism: "The millions of Gypsies of Eastern Europe have emerged as great losers from the overthrow of communism…(when) many of the economic and social protections that Gypsies enjoyed in Hungary, Romania and Czechoslovakia collapsed, permitting a revival of the open prejudice and persecution that have marked the history of the *Roma*." (NY Times International, 11/17/93 article by Henry Kamm, "End of Communism Worsens Anti-Gypsy Racism.")

My own observation was that in Romania Gypsies are universally despised and feared as thieves and criminals. For their part, the *Roma* resist integration, preferring to live in their own communities and by their own standards. Some have built large, ornate houses and are greatly envied by the general population for their display of wealth which, one is told, comes from stealing.

Romanian folk dancers

English teachers, Judith and Adi

Anne and U.S. visitors (in Maramureş traditional dress) Romanian host (in jeans)

Anne with older Romanian orphans in Tîrgu Mureş

Five and Ten Press Inc.

This is a small, independent press that publishes quality (in content, economically in presentation) paperback original works of fiction, non-fiction, and our specialty "factual fiction," in a variety of genres: memoirs, essays, short stories, novellas, miscellanies, and (once) poetry. All are published in limited first editions of from 400 to 600 copies, in 5" by 8" format that makes them convenient to carry in a coat pocket or purse while travelling on one conveyance or another. They rarely exceed 100 pages in length, so are not heavy to read in bed. The print font is fairly large, easy on the eyes.

Known as "Black Sheep Books," they are always priced at between $5 and $10, hence the name of the press. They are sold individually from our website (fiveandtenpress.com), by Internet booksellers such as amazon.com, and most successfully by subscription. Subscribers, of whom there are now more than 210, pay the press $25 in advance and receive, sight unseen, the next three or four publications. There are never any annoying charges for "shipping and handling," which for other presses are disguised profit centers. We mail by first class postage, which guarantees delivery.

Despite our stringent editorial quality control, we have thus far been able to publish 15 booklets. Nine have been authored by Robert V. Keeley, but we have also published six other writers, and there will be more of these in the future. The main criterion for publication is that the manuscript must show some wit, if possible a lot of wit. And secondly originality. Also, needless to say, readable style (not just "style"). Essentially we publish what mainstream (that is, commercial) publishers, magazines, newspapers, journals, and other outlets have no interest in and usually don't bother to respond to efforts to interest them.

If you would like to subscribe, just send us a check for $25 and make sure you enclose your mailing address. If you would like to buy individual copies, here is our list, with prices shown. There are no discounts, and no charges for postage. New subscribers receive a free "signing bonus" copy of their choice of any of these publications.

Five and Ten Press, Inc.
3814 Livingston Street N.W.
Washington, D.C. 20015-2803

Black Sheep Books—1995-2001

By Robert V. Keeley:

1. **D.C. Governance: It's Always Been a Matter of Race and Money.** 29 pages. December 1995. Second printing February 1996. $5. (Out of print. Photocopy only.) The fundamental problem of the nation's capital and a possible solution.

2. **Annals of Investing: Steve Forbes vs. Warren Buffett.** 49 pages. March 1996. $5. Second printing May 2000. Black humor. How not to—and how to—make money in the stock market.

3. **The File: A Princeton Memoir.** 96 pages. May 1996. $10. Nostalgia. Undergraduate escapades three decades—and many other changes—after F. Scott Fitzgerald.

4. **Essays Fast and Loose: A Christmas Miscellany.** 76 pages. November 1996. $7. The O.J. Simpson case solved, corporate culture criticized, health care reformed, the Olympics put down, Colin Powell questioned, Forbes revisited, and dancing for free cruises.

5. **Letters Mostly Unpublished.** 72 pages. March 1997. $5. Twenty-two items, mostly letters to the editor, most—and some of the best—of which never got into print.

6. **Essays Cold and Hot: A New Year's Potpourri.** 95 pages. January 1998. $10. Two terrible Supreme Court decisions, the condition of the nation's capital, a dysfunctional Senate, Andreas Papandreou of Greece, how to cure the common cold, and a Hollywood fantasy.

7. **MSS Revisited.** 72 pages. April 1998. $7. A Princeton undergraduate literary magazine recalled, with short stories by Jose Donoso, Walter Clemons, and R.V. Keeley.

8. **Three Sea Stories.** 102 pages. October 1999. $10. Memoirs. Lessons learned by a 16-year-old on a merchant marine voyage, by a 24-year-old on U.S. Coast Guard weather patrol, and by a 29-year-old in an encounter with a hospitalized sea captain.

9. **The Great Phelsuma Caper (A Diplomatic Memoir).** 140 pages. December 2000. $10. Macabre adventures with General Idi Amin Dada of Uganda, toilet training a pet bird, smuggling lizards, and other tall tales.

By other authors:

10. **Innocents of the Latter Day: Modern Americans Abroad.** 98 pages. May 1997. $10. By James W. Spain, a retired American ambassador. Eleven short stories about the Foreign Service set in South Asia, the Near East, and Africa.

11. **Creatures of the Earth and the Mind.** 60 pages. October 1998. $6. By Carl Coon, a retired American ambassador. Nine charming stories and essays about animal life, plus a profound essay about concepts underlying progressive humanism.

12. **My Commute.** 76 pages. December 1998. $10. By Alison Autobound Axel. Novella. A humorous account of contemporary corporate life from the point of view of a denizen of a cubicle at a large multinational to which she commutes daily. Dedicated to the downsized.

13. **Sic Transit.** 68 pages. December 1999. $6. By Carl Coon. Thirteen essays, some satirical, some humorous, some serious. Topics include power, the military mind, foreign affairs, Morocco, Nepal, marital relations, gender and generational differences, New York City, the Pope, and cyberspace.

14. **The Port of Missing Men (A Novel).** 253 pages. June 2001. $10. By Alain Prévost. Translated from the French by Ralph Woodward. Grégoire, a French student at Princeton University, matures and learns sophistication through interactions with his American fellow students and via an affair with his widowed Aunt Laura.

15. **Poetry Mostly Off The Beaten Track.** 56 pages. May 2001. $5. By Roy Herbert. A course in understanding poetry, citing great poems of the past. Includes some unpublished poems by the author.

Book design: Diahann Hill
Cover: Street leading to 14th century Saxon church in citadel town of
      Sighişoara, Transylvania
Backcover photograph: Peasant children riding to market, Kristen Heyniger